How to

INVEST

BEING R

Set up your investments, save money, get on with your life.

DAVID RYDER

Prospero Media Ltd.

PROSPERO MEDIA LTD.
4 Fenice Court
Phoenix Business Park
Eaton Socon, St. Neots
Cambridgeshire
PE19 8EP
United Kingdom

Email: enquiries@investwithoutbeingrippedoff.com
Website: investwithoutbeingrippedoff.com

First edition published in the United Kingdom by Prospero Media Ltd.

Paperback ISBN: 978-1-7394506-0-1
eBook ISBN: 978-1-7394506-1-8
Audiobook ISBN: 978-1-7394506-2-5

British Library Cataloguing Publication Data
A CIP catalogue record for this book can be obtained from the British Library.

Cartoons by Pete Dredge, https://petedredgecartoons.com

CONTENTS

To Claudia

She bought me a cigar last week and, while doing so, told me that I had to give her a dedication in this book.

She has also, over several years, applied her boot to my backside at just the right speed to spur me into action without causing irreparable damage to my metaphorical glutinous maximus.

ABOUT THIS BOOK

I want you to keep as much of your hard-earned money as you possibly can.

That's why, in this book, I:

- Use plain English
- Expose the horrendous rip-off that banks and investment companies perpetuate
- Show how I pay 90% less in fees than those rip-off merchants charge
- Have a very short list of investment websites that I'm happy to place my money with
- Take loads of the research and analysis that banks and investment companies generate, and use it **for free** in my own investments
- Go through an easy to follow, step-by-step process of setting up real investments with my own real money
- Minimise the amount of tax I have to pay on investments.

This book is accompanied by the website, InvestWithoutBeingRippedOff.com which is free to use and allows me to provide updates and additional information on everything, including how my actual investments are performing and what the genuine costs are that I'm incurring.

You can read the book from cover to cover, or dip into it to get the particular information you need, it's up to you.

Ultimately though, use this book to help you keep your money and have your investments work for you, not the other way around.

.

ABOUT ME

I'm a bit miffed

My 25 years' experience in the financial industry has left me deeply dismayed at the way ordinary investors, like you, are being ripped off.

I know because I was the person writing the performance reports you read, the "review" and "outlook" documents, the articles on setting up pensions and ISAs, and so on.

I did that for over 10 years for four massive financial institutions each of which manages billions of pounds of your money.

I'm doing myself out of a living by writing this book.

They won't employ me after this book comes out because I'm lifting the lid on what's going on. Maybe I'll end up delivering your groceries, who knows?!

However, it's become difficult for me to repeat the same excuses for the high fees (if you're paying more than 0.15% a year, you're probably being ripped off) and terrible performance (around 1 in 3,333 active funds beats the market).

The high fees for dire performance assures huge salaries for fund managers at the direct expense of your pension or nest egg.

Back to me

In my first 15 years in the industry, I worked as a financial publisher, editor and reporter.

During this period, I launched a series of corporate financial publications and made contributions to national newspapers and national radio.

Predicting the financial crisis

One of the publications I co-published predicted the financial crisis of 2007-09.

As early as 2003, we got a copy of that magazine into the hands of, then Junior Finance Minister, Ed Balls. In 2011, he had the decency to issue a public apology for not doing more.

In 2005, I appeared on the Stephen Nolan show on BBC Radio 5 Live and warned of the forthcoming financial crisis.

This was dismissed by the other guests on the show. One of those guests was an MP from Manchester who attacked me personally, accusing me of "talking down jobs", the exact opposite of what I was doing.

On the inside

A few years later, I joined a massive financial institution and began my time as a writer of reports and articles.

I was well paid and worked with, for the most part, excellent people who wanted to do the best for you and your fellow investors.

Unfortunately, the investment industry is predicated on charging a lot of money for a terrible service. No amount of effort from the minions can counteract that.

There is an alternative

I have used my own money to set up investments that copy the investment choices of the big financial institutions but for MUCH lower fees.

I share every step of how I do this in the following pages.

Don't let yourself be ripped off. Or miffed.

FOREWORD

By Jasmine Birtles, TV money guru and founder of MoneyMagpie.com

Did anyone teach you how to manage your money when you were growing up?

I'm guessing not.

I certainly didn't get any serious training. My parents taught me not to get into debt, so when I got my first credit card, I promptly spent an eye-watering amount that I couldn't pay back. Had I actually listened in maths lessons I would have realised the joy and wonder of compound interest and how it can amplify both your debts and your investments. As it was, I ended up learning the hard way, as so many do: watching my initial credit card borrowing mushroom into a mountain that took months to pay off.

But even once life had taught me the maths lesson of compound interest (good and bad) it took me quite a while to learn from life's psychology classes about the machinations of investment companies and "advisors".

The basics of investing are pretty straightforward on the whole: always have a mix of investments (I say "spread your bets"), practice "pound-cost averaging" (i.e., being regular with your investments) and generally keep your investments for a good, long time unless they prove themselves to be dogs.

So far so sensible.

But then you come to the end of a few years to find that the money you thought you were going to get from particular investments turns out to be some way short of your calculations. It's not that they have underperformed either, it's that some of the money has just "disappeared" along the way.

It's at that point, if you do a bit of digging, that you start to uncover the startling level of charges and fees that can be levied on your investments; fees that, apparently, you were told about in the small print, but for the life of you can't remember seeing or being told about.

It's basically robbery in a sharp suit, buttressed with posh, complicated words and phrases designed to obfuscate and make you, the investor, feel small and stupid so that you continue to pay up without questioning.

Happily, though, there are ways to protect your hard-earned money from the smooth-talkers while enabling your investments to grow the way they should.

This book gives you the secrets of how to do this.

In a simple, step-by-step format it shows you how to keep more of your money and stop it going into the pockets either of the financial companies or investment platforms or indeed the taxman who likes to take larger and larger chunks of our profits each year.

Happy, and profitable, investing!

GLOSSARY
Slightly tongue-in-cheek

A new pony for Cressida - What all those fees are paying for.

Absolute return – This is quite a tedious definition. There are others, later in this list, that are quite amusing. This ain't one of them. But here we go: Absolute return is the amount by which an investment rises or falls. This is different from relative return which is where the investment's change in value is measured against a benchmark. For example, if you invest £1,000 and it grows by 5%, taking it to £1,050, then your absolute return is 5%. If the benchmark, say the FTSE 100, has grown by 6%, then your relative return is -1%, i.e., 1% less than the benchmark.

Absolute return fund – A fund that doesn't have a benchmark. The idea is that the fund just returns growth. I'm not a fan because the ones I've seen have almost always delivered a really poor return.

Active – An active fund is one in which the fund manager and a cohort of analysts interfere with the fund to mess up the performance. They charge you, the investor, heavily for the privilege.

Advice – Advice from an Independent Financial Advisor (IFA) is whole-of-market advice that has no restrictions on the scope of funds to which your money can be allocated. "Advice" given by a "tied" or "restricted" advisor might have some positives and might, indeed, be from a decent, well-intentioned individual. However, if the said advisor is tied to a bank or investment company, they will only "advise" you according to what the company offers by way of its own limited and potentially expensive selection of investments.

AFM – See Authorised Fund Manager

Allocation – This refers to the different proportions of your money that go into different types of investment. For example, a 50% allocation to bonds means that half of your money will be used to buy bonds, while a 5% allocation to cryptocurrencies means that 5% of your money will vanish, never to be seen again.

Alternative – This refers to a bunch of investments that are neither shares (identify as "he"/"his") or bonds (identify as "she"/"hers") but other investments (identify as "eh?"/"huh?") such as property and gold.

Annuity – Ageuk.org.uk offers some good info on annuities. Its definition of an annuity is a product which "converts your savings into an annual pension, giving you a guaranteed income for life, or for a specific period." Finding a good annuity is a challenge because the people who sell them are, understandably, out to make a profit. Age UK has a short video on retirement tips from the excellent Paul Lewis, the host of BBC Radio 4's Moneybox. Paul Lewis (no relation to any other TV financial expert) is like a professorial uncle whom you wish you'd listened to more when you were growing up. You can see it here https://www.ageuk.org.uk/information-advice/money-legal/pensions/annuities/

Arbitrary – Done on a whim or with no apparent justification or foundation. A favourite process among some investment managers.

Asset – Something that is worth money and could be sold for cash. For example bonds, shares, or a young child who is wide-eyed, curious and could grow up to be a successful surgeon and pay for your retirement. A teenager who smells and doesn't get up before 11am is a social and financial liability.

Asset classes – Different types of investment such as shares and bonds. These can be divided by region or other classes e.g., Asian small company shares or North American government bonds.

Asset manager – Someone who lifts and separates assets (those of you of a certain age will get that reference). An asset manager is really just another name for someone who puts money into different investments. You can have active asset managers who interfere, ruin performance, and charge a high fee; or passive asset managers who set up assets to follow the performance of, say, the FTSE 100 or the price of gold, and then get out of the way, don't charge as much and deliver better performance.

Authorised Fund Manager (AFM) –The Financial Conduct Authority's definition of a fund management company that is legally ripping people off, as opposed to one that is doing so illegally.

Bad debt – This is debt that is expensive (i.e., with high interest rate charges) and which isn't for essentials. I think of hire-purchase for a TV, or credit card payments for a holiday as bad debt. Yes, we all need a holiday, but live within your means.

Belmarsh Prison – Retirement home for some financial professionals. It should be overflowing but, apparently, is not.

Benchmark – This is not the part of the park bench that the birds have bombed and which you don't want to sit on. It's another way of saying "target". For example, the benchmark for qualifying for the Olympic 100 metres final might be 10 seconds. And I might be a minute slower than that.

Best-in-class – This is a big, fat lie. It really means "investment choices that are the most expensive and which give some of the crappiest performance". When I get wind of anyone referring to their offering being "best-in-class", I skedaddle.

Bitcoin – See Cryptocurrency

Bonds – Genuine bonds are those sold by companies and governments to investors. They pay the investor an annual payment (see "coupon") and return the entire investment plus a bit to the investor after a fixed period of time. Note: these are different from the "bonds" that a bank or building society might sell in the UK, which are just saving accounts with rules. Those accounts are not bad in themselves, but it's important to note that their name is a misuse of genuine "bonds".

Britain's Got Talent – An oxymoron.

Capital Gains Tax (CGT) – This is when the taxman takes a chunk of any growth in value of your assets if he possibly can. I appreciate that nuclear missiles and Downing Street parties won't pay for themselves, so the money has to come from somewhere. However, CGT provides an excellent reason to make use of "tax wrappers" such as Individual Savings Accounts (ISAs) or Self-Invested Personal Pensions (SIPPs).

Cash buffer – Not some old fart who marches past wearing a top hat and falls asleep during debates in the House of Commons. A cash buffer is readily available cash that will cover short-term emergencies, preventing you from having to dip into your investments.

Charges – See Fees

Chartered IFA -An independent financial advisor who has done extra studies to attain "Chartered" status. This will make that person more expensive but might be an indicator of someone more dependable.

CGT – See Capital Gains Tax.

Costs – See Fees

Coupon – Not the fistful of torn-off slips of paper that the person in front of you in the supermarket queue is wasting your life with. A coupon is the annual payment paid out by bond issuers to the people who bought their bonds.

Cryptocurrency – (AKA **Crap**tocurrency) The quickest way to lose everything. Cryptocurrencies are just lines in a computer programme. They have no value, generate no returns, contribute nothing to anyone or anything. They're snake oil. They're also heavily promoted by various folk who have recognised that they can make loads of money by selling them to innocent investors. Remember that moment in the movie Indiana Jones and the Last Crusade where Indy is reaching into a crevice to try to retrieve the Holy Grail? His dad, Sean Connery, recognises that Indy has been seduced by the idea of eternal life but will get killed trying to retrieve the grail and says "Leave it, son". Don't be Indy, be Sean.

DFM – see Discretionary Fund Management or Belmarsh Prison.

Diversification – The act of not putting all your eggs in one basket. When I was at school, I didn't just annoy one teacher by mimicking them, I did it to most of them. That meant that I'd diversified the investment of my talent and would almost always be rewarded with a detention. Alternatively, you might want to think of it as investing in a range of shares and bonds perhaps with some alternatives as well. That's not as amusing, but it will get you home from school sooner.

Dividend – The share of profits which companies pay out to shareholders.

Draw down – To take out of. When you draw down from your Self-Invested Personal Pension (SIPP), you're taking money out of it. One can apply this concept to trousers.

Discretionary Fund Management (DFM) – This is where you grant complete freedom to the fund manager to make all sorts of stupid decisions to justify his fees and ruin your investment.

Environmental, Social and Governance Funds (ESG) – What you and I think of as "sustainable" investing. It considers the implications for the environment, the people involved, and the rules that are supposed to be followed. Much of this is meaningless noise (see Greenwashing) and is likely to remain so for a few years yet.

ESG – see Environmental, Social and Governance Funds

ESMA – see European Securities and Markets Association

ETF – see Exchange-Traded Fund

Ethereum – see Cryptocurrency or Self-flagellation

Equity – see Shares

European Securities and Markets Authority (ESMA) – A bunch of Continental Europeans who tear their hair out as they try to keep up with and regulate the financial shenanigans of fund managers and the like.

Exchange-Traded Fund (ETF) – In a conventional investment fund, you buy "units" in that fund (see "Unit" below). In an ETF, the fund is treated as if it is a company in which you can buy shares. The ETF is listed on a stock exchange (such as the London Stock Exchange). All the "company" is, is a selection of shares in other companies or holdings of bonds or other assets such as gold or property. The point to remember is that it tends to be a passive fund with relatively low fees, hence I've included them in my selection of low-cost funds.

Factsheet – This is a document that makes hilarious use of the word "fact". I should know, I used to write them. Investment companies, banks and whatnot have to provide them and they have to include information such as past performance and what they invest in. They're largely useless in my opinion.

FCA – See Financial Conduct Authority

Fees (costs, charges...) – The fund manager's favourite subject. These are what they charge in such a way that they look small (e.g., 1%) but are, in fact, what destroys your investment growth while guaranteeing the fund manager a six-figure salary plus bonus, pension and benefits.

Fellow IFA – An independent financial advisor.

Financial Advisor – See Independent Financial Advisor and Restricted Advisor.

Financial Conduct Authority (FCA) – The beleaguered UK financial watchdog that has scant chance of keeping up with the extremely well-paid and highly intelligent individuals who run investment companies and the like.

Financial Services Compensation Scheme (FSCS) – The UK government-backed guarantee of your money if the company you have the money with goes bust (à la Northern Rock). The company in question has to have a UK banking licence and the FSCS only covers you up to £85,000 under each respective banking licence (which can cover more than one company, e.g., Virgin Money, Clydesdale Bank and Yorkshire Bank are all under the same licence so that's a total of £85,000 that you might hold across all three). www.fscs.org.uk

Fixed income – You'd think it was what fund managers ensure they get from all the fees they charge despite your investments going down in value. It's not that. It's a general term used to cover bonds and similar investment types. The point being that most bonds pay a fixed annual return to people who've invested in those bonds no matter what's going on with interest rates, inflation and company profits. By contrast, shares tend to pay dividends based on annual profits, and that varies.

FTSE – This stands for Financial Times Stock Exchange. Just accept it. It's a bit like having to accept that Germans have six words for "the" (der, die, das, dem, den, des). Why? They just do. "Vorsprung durch technik" as they say.

FTSE 100, 250 and 350 – The FTSE 100 is the largest 100 companies whose shares you can buy and sell on the London Stock Exchange. The FTSE 250 is companies 101 to 350 (*not* the top 250). Just to make it fun, the FTSE 350 *is* the top 350 companies i.e., the combination of the FTSE 100 and the FTSE 250.

FTSE All-Share – This is all the shares listed on the London Stock Exchange, i.e., companies in which you and I can buy and sell shares.

Fund – A collection of investments in which investors can buy units (see "Units").

Fund manager – Fund managers of passive funds are people who tend not to charge too much for setting up and running a fund that tracks an index (e.g., the FTSE All-Share). Fund managers of active funds must never be referred to as "pinstriped criminals". That would be mean.

General Investment Account (GIA) – An ordinary investment account that you can set up on a platform (or directly with a bank if you want your financial face ripped off). It has no tax efficiency or tax wrapping such as is offered with a Self Invested Pension Plan (SIPP) or Individual Savings Account (ISA).

GIA – see General Investment Account

Gilts – Another name for UK government bonds. Today, they are just numbers on a screen as far as you and I are concerned. However, the physical bits of paper that those numbers represent used to have a silver gilt edging which showed that they were government bonds and, therefore, supposedly less risky. I could make a quip about a different spelling and how it might apply to active fund managers, but I think you've got the idea by now.

Government bonds – Guess what, these are bonds issued (sold) by governments. They're also referred to as "govvies" and sovereign bonds (because they're issued on behalf of the sovereign/state government).

Govvies – See Government bonds

Gross – The number before fees or other deductions are charged. Nothing to do with the character of, or salaries paid to, any financial service industry executives.

Hedging – Counterbalancing or reducing the exposure to risk. For example, if you think your spouse won't like the birthday present you've got for them, you might hide a second back-up present to ensure that you can continue to occupy the bed between midnight and 7am. In investment terms, you might keep more cash if you think share prices are going to fall so that you don't lose too much money. Frankly, I think the birthday present thing is more important because you can ignore your investments for a year and both they and you will benefit. Try that with your spouse and you'll soon find out how comfortable or otherwise the couch is.

High-yield – Yield is another word for return. High-yield just means high return, but it also carries the almost certain likelihood of higher risk. Hence "high-yield" bonds are also referred to as "junk" or "sub-investment" grade bonds coz they are highly risky.

IFA – See Independent Financial Advisor

Independent Financial Advisor (IFA) – A UK advisor who can advise on the full range of investments available to retail investors like you and me.

Index-linked – A fancy way of saying that it roughly follows or allows for changes in the rate of inflation. The index to which something is linked is likely to be the Consumer Price Index or the Retail Price Index, both of which are (not-entirely-accurate) measures of the rate of inflation.

Inflation – The rate at which prices are increasing, usually measured on an annual basis.

Investment Association – A coven of wizened incubi who meet under a full moon to fashion new and colourful PowerPoint presentations that enchant investors and make their savings vanish in a puff of fees i.e., the investment firms' trade group.

Investment-grade – A short way of saying "bonds that carry a lower level of risk".

Instrument – A jargony way of saying "type of investment" or "investment thing".

Investment manager – See fund manager. They're close enough for the purposes of this book.

Investment Trust – This works in much the same way as a fund in that it, the trust, owns a bunch of shares or bonds or alternatives. The difference is that, instead of buying units in a fund, a trust is set up like a company in which you buy shares.

Individual Savings Account (ISA) – An account in which you can keep cash or buy investments and for which any profits made cannot be taxed. Yay! UK only I'm afraid.

ISA – see Individual Savings Account.

International Securities Identification Number (ISIN) – This is the unique collection of letters and numbers that each fund has and which I use to find the funds I want to invest in when I'm using an investment website or "platform".

ISIN – International Securities Identification Number.

Junk bonds – See High-Yield.

Key Investor Information Document (KIID) – Another largely pointless document that fund managers have to produce to provide a veneer of honesty about what they're fund invests in.

KIID – see Key Investor Information Document.

Laughably unlikely – See Outperformance

Liquidity – How easy or difficult it is to turn something into cash. Your savings are liquid because you can get the cash out of them relatively quickly. Your house is illiquid because it would take time and hassle to sell it i.e., to convert it to cash. Your smelly teenage son hasn't seen any cleansing liquid since the age of 13; thoroughly illiquid.

Marginal tax rate – This is the amount of tax you pay "on an additional pound of income". At the time of writing in 2023, UK marginal tax rates were:

Band	Taxable income	Tax rate
Personal Allowance	Up to £12,570	0%
Basic rate	£12,571 to £50,3070	20%
Higher rate	£50,271 to £125,140	40%
Additional rate	over £125140	45%

You can find the updated numbers at www.gov.uk/income-tax-rates

Market – For investments, this term is misused quite a lot. When folk say "the market has risen" they're actually talking nonsense. I've never been to a market and seen it levitate. Don't get me wrong, I'd love to see that. While I wait for that, I can tell you that the market is, in fact, the virtual (i.e., online) marketplace in which shares and bonds are bought and sold. When folk say the market is "up", "down", "nervous", "succulent" (I've never heard them call it succulent, but it would be just as nonsensical), they're referring to the general mood across buyers and sellers or the overall value of shares or bonds e.g., "the market is up" means that the prices of shares have risen.

Model portfolio – This is the target portfolio that I want my portfolio to be as similar to as possible. Think of me as the model portfolio and Henry Cavill as longing to look more like me.

Mutual fund – This is normally what you're referring to when you say "fund". It's a collection of investments in which us retail investors can buy a bit of that fund i.e., a "unit". The price of a unit will fall or rise in line with the value of the investments that the fund owns.

Naked model at the gym – You're reading the wrong book. But let me have a copy when you find it.

National Insurance (NI) – A UK tax that is, in theory, used to pay for the NHS, unemployment benefit, sickness and disability allowances, and the UK state pension.

Net – What's left after costs etc. have been removed. Net performance is the only number that matters, which is why active fund managers will move Heaven and Earth to avoid telling you what the net performance numbers on your investments are.

NI – see National Insurance

OCF – See Ongoing Charges Figure

Ongoing Charges Figure (OCF) – This is what you get charged for the running of a fund. It is similar to the Total Expense Ratio (TER). I only refer to the OCF, and not the TER, in this book to keep things simple LOL. The point being that I want the right fund covering the right asset class and charging me as low an OCF as possible.

Outperformance – Snake oil, Scotch mist, pipe dream. It's what active fund managers say they "strive for", "aim to achieve", "design their funds to deliver" but NEVER guarantee and very, very rarely actually achieve. I understand how unlikely it is to get outperformance, hence I want reasonable performance in line with the general improvement in the values of shares, bonds and alternatives.

Overperformance – See Outperformance.

Passive – Not active i.e., a fund that just aims to follow the performance of, say, the FTSE 100, UK government bonds, or the price of fish. Passive funds are much cheaper than active funds because you're not subsidising anyone's private yacht.

Performance – The profits or losses on an investment over a period of time. A cynic might suggest that "performance" is what fund managers put on to convince you that they're overpriced, underperforming funds aren't crap.

Platform – A website on which I can set up an investment account and buy the funds that I want for my investment portfolio.

Portfolio – Just a posh way of saying "collection" or "group". Hence you can have a portfolio of your artwork, a portfolio of the investments you hold or a portfolio of the people you offended last night by going too far with your toilet humour.

Pound-cost averaging – Drip feeding. Rather than paying a large sum of money (e.g., £10,000) into a fund at once, you might pay it into a fund a bit at a time (e.g., £1000 a month for 10 months). The theory is that this makes your portfolio less likely to suffer from a sudden drop in the value of investments shortly after you've made a large investment. The counter argument is the transaction and tax fees that will be incurred every time an investment is made. My preference is to set up my investment portfolio up front with low-cost funds using whatever money I can afford to put into investments, and then add to it on a regular basis. I cover this in more detail in the main body of the book.

RDR – see Retail Distribution Review

Rebalancing – Adjusting a portfolio of investments to bring it back in line with the model portfolio that you're copying.

Restricted advisor – An appropriately named person who should be restricted from giving you advice on where to invest because they are only going to point to the funds of the company that pays their salary. This is genuinely sad because I know a lot of restricted advisors and the majority of them are really decent folk who have their hands tied by their employers.

Retail Distribution Review – This was the painfully overdue review of how and what fund managers and advisors charged the vulnerable retail investor. It had a very positive effect by forcing banks and investment houses to reveal what they charged and how they charged it. That has brought about some price competition, but there's still plenty of room for improvement.

Returns – See Performance

Risk – A good thing if used properly. You cannot avoid taking some risk, nor should you try. Holding cash carries risk as it gets eroded by inflation and your sneaky teenage kid. The key is to take the right amount of risk for you.

Risk-rated funds – Funds that have been designed to carry a set level of risk, e.g. lower-risk, medium-risk and higher-risk.

S&P 500 – The US equivalent of the FTSE 100. The S&P 500 is an index of the 500 largest companies that you can buy and sell shares in in the US. This index is put together by Standard & Poor's, hence the "S&P" bit.

Self-flagellation – The physical equivalent of buying cryptocurrency.

Shares (stocks, equity) – A bit of a company. If you own a share in a company, you are entitled to a share of that company's profits when they are distributed as dividends. Not all companies issue dividends (Amazon has never paid a dividend). However, your ability to hold onto that share means that the value of your share could rise or fall with the fortunes of the company.

Self-Invested Personal Pension (SIPP) – This is a tax-efficient way of investing the in UK. Money put into a SIPP is not subject to tax. Money taken out of (drawn down from) a SIPP is subject to tax but at potentially favourable rates.

SIPP – see Self-Invested Personal Pension.

Sovereign bonds – See government bonds.

Stock – See Shares

Stock market – Where shares in companies are bought and sold. This is largely just done electronically now. The days of Dan Ackroyd and Eddie Murphy in a trading pit partaking in open outcry trading are now few and far between. This form of verbal abuse and aggression has transferred to slow-moving traffic on urban roads, especially during rush hour.

Stock-picking – The art and science of selecting individual company shares to invest in rather than buying funds that are themselves invested in lots of different company shares. Successful stock-picking is difficult but not impossible. Read Robbie Burns' *The Naked Trader* if you think it's for you.

Store of value – Something that holds its value even as inflation or other factors change. For example, gold has traditionally been a store of value as it's price has tended to rise or fall as inflation has risen or fallen. This is less evident these days.

Tax – Like death but sooner.

Tax wrapper – A way of keeping or investing money that is tax-efficient and restricts what access, if any, the taxman can have.

TER - See Total Expense Ratio

Tied advisor – See Restricted Advisor

Tiers – Layers. I've arranged my portfolios in layers, "tiers", according to how much money I might have to invest.

Total Expense Ratio (TER) – This is a calculation of how much it's likely to cost the investor to own a share in a fund. For example, if you invest £10,000 and the TER is 1%, you can expect to pay £100 a year.

Treasuries – See government bonds

Tracking – Following. A "tracking fund" or "tracker" might track the FTSE 100. It would be designed to go up 1% when the FTSE 100 goes up 1% and go down 1% when the FTSE 100 goes down 1%.

Tracking error – This measures how closely a tracker follows its target. A tracking error of 0 means that the tracker fund has exactly matched the performance of what it's tracking. For example, if a FTSE 100 Tracker fund exactly matches the rises and falls in the FTSE 100 then that tracker fund has a tracking error of zero. No tracking fund has such an accurate tracking error. The vast majority of passive funds tracked their targets to with 0.75% in the financial year-ending April 2021 according to the FCA; that's very close tracking and indicates performance of the tracker that is very similar to the respective targets.

Underlying funds – The funds contained within a portfolio.

Underperformance – What most active funds give you in return for paying high fees. For example, if the FTSE 100 has gone up 1% but your active fund investment only rose by 0.5%, the fund has underperformed the FTSE 100 by 0.5%. And that's before the active fund rips off another 1% or more from you.

Units – A piece of, or a share in, a fund. If the overall value of a fund is £100 and it has 100 units available to buy, you can reckon on paying about £1 for one unit in that fund.

Volatility – What happens to a fund manager's face when you ask why they charge such high fees for such crappy performance. It's also another way of saying the speed with which prices move up and down. Highly volatile means large and swift upward and downward swings in price.

Watchdog – I have two dogs. One's called Timex, the other's called Rolex. They're watchdogs. The FCA is the UK's investment industry watchdog.

Weighted – The proportion of something is the weighting. For example, if I have a portfolio worth £100 with a 10% weighting to bonds and a 90% weighting to shares then I have £10 in bonds and £90 in shares.

Whole-of-market – All the funds in which retail investors can buy units.

Wrapper – Not a tiresome male who can't play instruments, write music or sing, and who feels disenfranchised by society—hence his need to shoot other men and molest women—that's clearly a different spelling. No, for the purposes of this book, a wrapper is a barrier to the taxman. ISAs and SIPPs are tax-wrapped investments.

PART ONE

Why I've written this book

1. Who this book is for
2. High fees, dreadful service
3. Real advice or glorified sales?
4. Horrific real-life example of "advice"
5. Genuine advice

1 Who this book is for

My primary purpose is to try to help ordinary folk who don't have much knowledge about investments.

Ask yourself these questions:

- Are you at all intimidated by the world of investments?
- Do you want to spend as little time as possible thinking about or working on your investments?
- Do your eyes glaze over whenever someone mentions finance or investments?
- Would you prefer to just set up your investments and get on with your life?
- Do you fail to understand some of the terminology used in finance?
- Do you rely on your bank or your friends to advise you on how to invest?
- Do you have zero qualifications in finance and investments, and intend to keep it that way?
- Do you just want a simple, low-cost way of building your nest egg/pension?

If you answered "yes" to any of these questions then this book is designed for you. The industry refers to you as an "unsophisticated" or "retail" investor, which is understandable but slightly condescending. I think a more appropriate definition is "normal human being".

As a normal human being/retail investor, you are vulnerable to the lies, manipulation and general aura of superiority that so many banks and investment firms are guilty of.

I'll lead you, step-by-step, through my process of setting up investments in a low-cost, risk-appropriate way. I'll use plain

English and even some humour here and there so that you don't get bored or overwhelmed.

This book is not for would-be stock-pickers

If you fancy yourself as a budding stock-picker and are excited by the idea of researching companies, buying and selling them and getting into the nitty gritty of investment, then this book is not for you.

The best book I've come across for stock pickers is *The Naked Trader* by Robbie Burns. Robbie is totally honest and transparent about what he does and how he does it. He's also a self-made ISA millionaire.

I've met him and I trust him. If you want to do all the complicated research and investment stuff and don't know where to start, buy *The Naked Trader*. And, no, I don't get any commission. In fact, he has no idea that I've made this recommendation.

I've set up a website to accompany this book

If I talk about things that you don't understand or if there are things that I've not covered, you can visit the supporting website where you'll find tons more info and an opportunity to submit queries.

Remember, there's no such thing as stupid questions, only a lack of knowledge. The website address is InvestWithoutBeingRippedOff.com. It's at the bottom of every other page of this book.

Bottom line

I want to help people who want relatively simple investments that don't charge too much and that don't offer what they can't deliver. I'm thinking of people who have more important things to do than worry about investments.

2 High fees, dreadful service

Ordinary folk like you are being ripped off when it comes to investments.

Mix of shares, bonds, etc.

Almost all fund managers, banks and investment houses are pretty good at making sure that their multi-asset funds have a decent mix of assets. That's because it doesn't stop them from

Beating the banks (and investment companies)

	What I want	What is offered
Mix of assets	Appropriate	Appropriate
Fees	As low as possible	As high as possible
Performance	In line with markets	Worse than markets
My level of worry	As low as possible	Unnecessarily high

selecting expensive underlying funds that generate lots of fees for them.

Fees

Some fees are inevitable: a service should be paid for. But I want to pay as little as possible while still setting up a balanced, sensible and appropriate set of investments ("portfolio") for me.

Performance

The evidence shows that "active" funds' performance after fees is, all too often, dreadful.

I want to spend as little time as possible managing my investments

Ideally, I'd like to spend no more than a few hours setting my investments up and then, say, a couple of hours once a year making sure that they're on track. I also don't want to think about why my investments are underperforming the market. A reasonable return that tracks the market is fine by me.

Hence you will discover:

- How people are, as far I can see, being ripped off
- How I use the expensive research conducted by lots of banks and investment companies for my own portfolios
- How I draw on my industry experience to select low-cost providers
- All my research and findings and how I use them
- The entire step-by-step process I use to set up and manage low-cost but carefully chosen investments.

While I have many years' experience as an investment professional, I am not a financial advisor. The information contained in this book is not a substitute for advice from an Independent Financial Advisor (IFA) who can be aware of your circumstances.

My 25 years in finance

I have worked in the investment industry, one way or another, for more than 25 years. For more than half of that, my role was as an "Investment Writer" i.e., the person who writes the reports on why performance hasn't been as good as it should have been; commentary on national and global events and how they affect investments; and what to expect in the coming months and years.

What I've seen and been required to do within the finance industry has left me hugely sceptical of the industry's general ability to prioritise the interests of the average individual who wants to invest.

In fact, I would say that the majority of the senior people running financial organisations prioritise making as much money as possible, including from the unwitting and vulnerable ordinary man or woman on the street.

That's why I pulled my pension and other investments out of various employer programmes and managed them all myself. Rather than paying an annual fee of up to 2.20%, I've set up portfolios with funds that charge an average of between 0.08% and 0.05%, that's more than 27-times cheaper.

An exorbitant fee for dire returns

I have no problem with a company making a profit for services rendered. That's as it should be. After all, without a profit, the firm wouldn't exist and the service might be harder or impossible to get.

What I object to is charging too much or providing a poor service. In my opinion, as far as investments are concerned, large swathes of the finance industry are guilty on both counts.

Things were even worse in the UK before 2013. This was before the law was changed as a result of the Retail Distribution Review (RDR) which, finally, recognised that ordinary investors were being royally conned. Fees were not only being hidden, but far too high and everything was cloak-and-dagger.

The main difference now is that fees are out in the open. As a result, banks and investment companies have had to come clean about what they charge. But prices are still far too high.

Damning assessment from the Financial Conduct Authority (FCA)

There's still a very long way to go before the industry puts the investor first. The industry watchdog, the Financial Conduct Authority (FCA) had the following to say about the effect of the RDR:

> "The financial advice market is improving...slowly. We think more can be done to support consumers."
>
> *Source: Evaluation of the impact of the Retail Distribution Review and the Financial Advice Market Review 3 December 2020, FCA.org.uk*

That is a very diplomatic way of putting it. What it boils down to is that most banks and investment firms still charge lots of money for dreadful returns.

Bottom line

Most banks, fund managers and investment companies charge too much and deliver too little.

3 Real advice or glorified sales?

Avoid "tied" or "restricted" advisors

There aren't enough Independent Financial Advisors (IFAs) who offer "whole-of-market" advice in the UK (see the *Financial Planning Today* article, "76% of IFAs plan to retire in the next 10 years", 22 May 2023.

By whole-of-market, I mean those who can take into account all the investments that are available to a retail investor like you or me.

By contrast, there are plenty of "advisors" who work for banks and investment firms. These advisors are called "tied" advisors because they are, surprise surprise, tied to a single bank or investment firm and are able to sell only the limited range of investments that these institutions offer.

I've worked with plenty of tied advisors in a couple of very large, very reputable companies. I've found most of them to be decent folk who want to help their clients.

But they're tied. The ONLY investments into which they will ever advise you to put your money are those offered by the company for which they work. This means that your money won't be allocated across the broadest range of investments.

Rip-Off Tip-Off

I would only consider getting advice from a whole-of-market Independent Financal Advisor.

Sales patter (splatter?)

Tied advisors will use phrases like "best-in-class". This is an excuse for not offering a really good selection. It's a phrase that cannot easily be defined, which is why they can get away with using it.

In one of the places I worked, there were fewer than 10 portfolios into which all clients' money would be invested; that's a choice of 10 with what were described as best-in-class underlying funds. And, like many other companies, they had to close one or two of

Stockings
5 gifts / Marin
Alison b'day
Bernard : biscuits
Marie : J. Malone body ~~cream~~ lotion
David b'day – biscuits posh
David + Claudia christmas
Jane Taylor b'd

th worse performance than cash sa

Al rtfolios offered by this co s. As is usually the case for investors high fees and del

On tied investors claiming tha they're on a salary and dor work in order to inflate thei

I'm sons:

- A are legally obliged to p client
- T e choice of funds that th ey into. IFAs have no su

An I and £1,500 for a comp cation of investments with r red for at least one year. A chance that they're ove

Wh funds?

Befo terms because they are ce tive funds; and the ones th ve seen, offer better returns for me, the at lower costs i.e., passive funds. I give further explanation in the Glossary and in chapter 17.

An actively managed fund is one in which people conduct research and analysis with the supposed intention of beating the market i.e., earning higher returns than you would by investing in cheaper, passive funds.

Based on that activity, their gut feel and what they've had for breakfast, they choose what to invest in and change their selection when they feel it appropriate.

As a result of this labour-intensive activity, the fees are almost always higher than those you would pay with passive funds but the performance tends to be worse, not better, not even the same, worse.

A passively managed fund is one that aims to follow the ups and downs of an asset, such as the price of gold or oil; or the ups and downs of a collection of companies, such as the FTSE 100 (the largest 100 UK-based companies that you and I can buy shares in) or the S&P 500 in the US (the largest 500 companies in the US that you and I can buy shares).

Because there's no need for analysis or research, the fees tend to be low and the performance more or less follows whatever is going on in the asset or index in question.

Discretionary Fund Management (DFM)

Discretionary Fund Management (DFM) is where a highly paid investment or banking company says "Give us control of your money. It's much too complicated for you to understand. We'll make all the decisions and charge you a modest fee."

If you have gazillions to invest, this might make some sense. But I've only ever seen it fail. The fee sounds modest because it's something like 1% but that equates to loads of money only to be sent newsletters and webinar invitations telling you all sorts of financial irrelevances that never quite explain why they keep underperforming their own benchmarks or cheaper passive funds.

Profit is the fund manager's priority

As I've said before, I don't think there's anything wrong with someone delivering a decent service and charging a fair fee. If they don't make a profit, they won't stay in business and I need fund managers to stay in business so that I can invest.

That said, in my experience, the returns generated by active fund managers is dreadful and the fees are far too high.

Again, it's not just me who thinks this

I recently had coffee with some former colleagues. During the conversation, they all reiterated that they would never invest in the very funds that they were working for.

Fudging the truth

The banks and investment companies I don't like, go on and on about their research and analysis facilities, their skilled staff, their network of offices and the range of funds they offer, etc.

The more they talk about all these things, the more likely they are to be charging a lot of money for a poor investment service.

If they do mention performance or returns, they talk about "gross" returns or just "returns". What this means is that they're talking about the returns they've generated BEFORE they subtract their fees and charges.

They hate telling you the net returns because it reveals how bad the returns are that you're getting.

For example, if their returns have been 3.0% over the past year, but they charge you 1.0% a year, you're left with a 2.0% return. They've just helped themselves to a third of all the growth of your investments in that year. Take into account the compounding (see chapter 9) and that chunk of fees makes a massive difference to how long it will take for you to reach your investment goals.

Their gross returns are completely irrelevant to me. I have no interest in them. I only care about the actual returns they've generated for me i.e., net returns. If those net returns are lower than the net returns I could have earned with a cheaper, simpler alternative, then why would I pay the higher fees?

Excuses, excuses

Some of the reasons (excuses?) they'll give for not disclosing net fees include:

- The charges are different for each customer, so it's "simpler" or "fairer" to provide the gross numbers
- There are different charges according to the funds being used
- The charges are taken at different times, so it varies depending on when the return is measured....

I'm not persuaded by any of these points.

If a company is able to manage lots of money, and if it has all those skilled people and research and analysis facilities, and if it's so good at charging its fees quickly and efficiently, why can't they just tell me what return they've earned for me with equal speed and efficiency?

Avoid "Rolls-Royce service" or "best-in-class" investments

If a company claims to offer a Rolls-Royce service or best-in-class investments, or uses language that is technical and full of jargon, I walk away.
I don't need and certainly can't justify the expense of a Rolls-Royce or any similarly unnecessarily costly thing. I just want a simple investment portfolio that's appropriate for me, cheap to run and largely takes care of itself without me doing much.

And best-in-class is often the excuse they use for not offering a choice across the whole of the market. My research of dozens of investment service providers and the selection of funds they tend to offer, strongly indicates that a company not offering whole-of-market often promotes its own expensive funds rather than the cheaper alternatives that offer much the same outcome.

Rip-Off Tip-Off

For me, "best-in-class" means "worst-for-me"

I need fair returns AFTER fees and charges, for a fair charge. If that means the equivalent of a reliable two-door Japanese run-around, then so be it. Just get me from A to B safely and without charging me more than is fair.

Decent people working for questionable companies

A poor investment selection is offered by some of the more reputable and (relatively) decent firms.

I know from direct experience that many of the tied advisors working for at least one of these companies found this demoralising and frustrating because it made it difficult for those tied, but well-intentioned, advisors to support the clients the way they wanted to.

The tied advisors were largely decent people trying to do a decent job in difficult circumstances.

Unfortunately, there are plenty of tied advisors working for investment firms who, while charming, are focused only on the money they can make for themselves. In theory, they are required by law to act in the best interests of their clients. Many, but not all, do so, as you'll see in the next chapter.

Bottom line

Most banks, fund managers and investment companies use all sorts of fancy words, charts and presentations to keep investors' money so that they can continue to charge too much and deliver too little.

4 Horrific real-life example of "advice"

There's one investment company I have in mind that has developed, shall I say, a "muddy" reputation. It's not alone by any means, so it would be unfair of me to name it. For the purposes of this explanation, we'll call it "Posh Investments".

It's a very large investment firm with all the branding and trappings of what appears to be a reputable company. I would never put my money anywhere near it though.

Here's why.

While I was working for another very large investment company, which we'll call "Big Money", many of Big Money's tied advisors (i.e., salespeople because they weren't independent) were approached by Posh Investments to come and work for Posh as tied advisors and earn a lot more money if they also brought their clients over with them.

Many of my former colleagues at Big Money saw this approach for what it was - an opportunity for tied advisors to make a lot of money for themselves (the salespeople and Posh Investments) at the expense of their clients. But some of Big Money's advisors were so fed up or greedy that they joined Posh Investments.

As soon as they'd joined Posh Investments, they contacted all of the clients they'd had at Big Money (which was against their contractual agreements but that didn't discourage them) and told those clients that they had a better opportunity for them at Posh.

What they had sounded better but was, in fact, much worse for many of their clients.

Instead of putting up with the high fees and awful performance at Big Money, the clients could come over to Posh Investments where the advisor would put all the client's money into a fund which only invested in bonds.

The fund would charge lower annual fees and be likely to offer a more reliable (if potentially lower) return for the client.

Quite understandably, the client would hear "lower fees" and "more reliable return". That would solve the two big complaints they had with Big Money, right?

Wrong.

Yes, the fund would charge lower annual fees and have a less variable return BUT, there are two key points that were not made clear to the investors.

1. Upfront fees of 5%

The client would incur chunky fees upfront. Posh Investments' advisors were incentivised to bring in as many clients as possible to generate as many fees as possible. That would contribute to the massive profits of Posh Investments while lining their advisors' pockets.

2. Tax on gains made to date

The investor could be hit by a massive tax bill.

While the money is invested, the taxman isn't terribly interested because the value can go up and down. That makes taxing it too much of a headache for everyone.

However, when you take money out of an investment, this is the taxman's opportunity to pounce. (I talk about how UK investors can limit tax on investments in Part 6 - Tax-efficient investing in the UK). If your investment has gone up in value, the taxman can ask you for a big chunk of the gains you've made.

The numbers

Here's how it might work in principle with some hypothetical numbers. Imagine you fall for Posh Investment's cunning wheeze and transfer your entire investment nest egg from Big Investments (this is what was actually happening by the way).

Let's say you've been saving up all your life, that you're in your late 60s and your general investment account has reached £250,000. The total amount of money you put in over the years was, say £125,000.

That would mean that £125,000 came from growth in the value of your investments over time. It's this £125,000 of growth that would be subject to tax if it had not been covered by a tax wrapper such as a SIPP or ISA.

The taxman sees this (you have to tell him by law) and asks for a Capital Gains Tax (CGT) payment. The rate of CGT varies from country to country. In the UK it ranges from between 10% and 28% (at the time of writing in 2023), with no tax to pay on the first £6,000 (it's just been slashed from £12,300).

In other words, the taxman wants a chunk (between 10% and 28%) of the £119,000 (£125,000 of gains minus the £6,000 allowance).

Here's roughly what this might mean

You had £250,000 with Big Money.
You withdraw all £250,000 of it to put into Posh Investments.
You put this money into Posh Investments which takes a 5% up-front fee (that's not the highest up-front fee that the real-life company I have in mind actually charges).
That's a massive up-front fee of £12,500 wiped off your nest egg.

> At the end of the financial year, if the investment was not in a tax-wrapped investment, the taxman could step in and ask you for between 10% and 28% of £119,000, i.e., between £11,900 and £33,320.

After Posh and the taxman (sounds like a really bad 1980s band...it kind of is) have taken their respective chunks, you could be left with between £225,600 and £204,180 of your £250,000 pension pot.

In this example, by moving to what seemed like a sensible investment encouraged by a "professional advisor", you'd have been fleeced to the value of between £12,500 and £45,820.

Let's assume that the hypothetical numbers I've come up with are wrong by, say, 50%. You'd still be facing a loss of between £6,000 and £22,000. It will take years to recoup that loss just as you're heading into retirement and no longer earning.

Not all investment firms are this bad. But it shows just how careful you have to be.

Bottom line

No matter what regulations are put in place, ordinary investors will always be vulnerable to companies and individuals whose number one priority is to make as much money as possible for themselves. It's not all of them, but it is far too many.

5

Genuine advice

The IFAs who offer whole-of-market coverage are not tied or restricted to what one bank or investment firm offers. They look across the entire range of what's available and try to pick out what should work for you in your unique circumstances.

They charge for their services and rightly so. IFAs have told me that, at the time of writing, they charge approximately £200 per hour with the expectation that they'll spend around three hours with you and then charge for another four hours' work. That hourly rate goes up to £250/£300 per hour for a chartered IFA.

Unhelpfully, they tend not to be interested in investors with less than an overall total of £100,000 to invest. Don't be surprised then, if you have to fork out £1,000-£1,500 for upfront financial advice.

Not all advisors are equal

A wealthy friend of mine faced this with an IFA who wanted 1% of his pension pot annually for what seemed to me to be not much value.

After a year or two of this, my friend agreed with my perspective and stopped the ongoing advice as it wasn't adding much value and certainly wasn't worth 1% of his pension pot each year.

The problem is finding a good IFA with experience and total integrity. If your investments are set up properly in the first place, you shouldn't need much advice after that unless your circumstances change. I start to question some IFAs when they want to charge an annual fee for ongoing advice.

Some tips on finding a decent IFA

Here's what a qualified and trustworthy advisor said to me: "A good financial advisor will get you some good returns. A great one will help you achieve your goals and build a plan for you to do that."

IFAs don't just cover investment decisions. They also provide things like inheritance tax planning (very worthwhile) and insurance. For some reason, they insist on calling insurance "protection" which always puts me in mind of an activity with a rather different risk-reward consideration.

And we're back in the room. So how do you find a decent IFA?

You could consider one that's "chartered" or a "fellow". This means that they have put in the graft to get additional qualifications and that they have relevant experience that's been verified.

Better still, you could look for a chartered IFA firm i.e., one in which the whole business sets its standards around experienced and highly qualified advisors.

Here are some questions I might ask

- Please provide three references of people you've provided professional advice to in the past 6 months whom I can speak to.
- What is your hourly rate?
- What is the maximum number of hours you'd expect to need to provide a complete financial review for me?
- What is the median OCF of the funds that you recommend for the following asset classes:
    - ◊ UK All Share
    - ◊ US All Share
    - ◊ Global Shares
    - ◊ UK Corporate Bonds
    - ◊ US Corporate Bonds
    - ◊ etc. (see Part Five for more asset classes)

None of these points guarantees a decent advisor but they should help to reduce the chances of ending up with a mediocre one.

Rip-Off Tip-Off

I'll put these into a form with more detail on the website. It will provide clarity on how those questions, and their respective answers, might help to provide some context on the advisor.

The "model" portfolios I use

A "model" portfolio is another way of saying "target" or "ideal" mix of investments that I can copy.

In real life, you can never precisely match the model, but you can get as close as possible to the model portfolio that most closely reflects the levels of risk and diversification that are most appropriate for you.

For example, if I'm in my 20s and won't need to access my investments for decades, my target or model portfolio might be dominated by higher-risk investments such as shares in companies.

By contrast, if I'm uncomfortable with risk, the target or model portfolio that I'd emulate might have a large proportion of government bonds.

With this in mind, I've created some simple model portfolios that I am moving my money into.

I cover all this in Part Seven - Using their research. In short I

- Collect the results of over 80 investment companies' research
- Copy the average allocation for Lower-Risk, Medium-Risk and Higher-Risk investment portfolios

- Choose low-cost passive funds that deliver very similar allocations but for MUCH lower fees.

In other words, I take what they do well, namely research, and replace what they do badly, selecting funds to put money into.

This is not a replacement for independent financial advice, but it is designed to give some insight so that you might feel less helpless and less ignorant when sitting in front of an IFA, blindly trusting every word they say.

Bottom line

I can't give advice and that's as it should be. However, my experience might give you some useful background for when you make investment decisions.

PART TWO

The Rip-Off

6

The FCA's damning assessment

The Financial Conduct Authority (FCA), the investment industry's watchdog, issued a damning assessment of what fund managers charge their retail customers.

Published in July 2021, it's entitled the Authorised fund managers' assessments of their funds' value. You can download it here: https://www.fca.org.uk/publications/multi-firm-reviews/authorised-fund-managers-assessments-their-funds-value.

Here are some of the things the FCA had to say:

"Authorised Fund Managers (AFMs) often made assumptions that they could not justify to us."

My translation: Often, what they're saying isn't true.

> *"Many firms did not properly apply some of the minimum considerations, including performance and approved fund management costs."*
> ***My translation:*** They were being dishonest when describing the returns they'd deliver on your investments and what they'd charge you.
>
> *"When considering a fund's performance, many firms did not consider what the fund should deliver given its investment policy, investment strategy and fees."*
> ***My translation:*** They were being either lazy or downright dodgy when talking about the returns that they indicated they would achieve.

Now sit down, take a deep breath and read this bit carefully (I've emboldened the key words):

> *"This was particularly apparent for funds that charged a fee commensurate with active management (i.e. with the aim of outperforming market returns), and were managed with the aim of outperformance, but had a more limited stated objective of achieving 'long-term capital growth', or similar wording. Because markets have generally been rising in recent years, approved* **fund managers** *with these funds* **often assessed the funds' performance** *consideration* **as providing value even where they have underperformed the markets** *in which they are invested. It is important to stress that funds which generate positive returns do not necessarily deliver good value."*
> **My translation**: The higher the fees you pay, the more likely that you'll get dire returns.
> **AND**
> They take credit for rises in value that had nothing to do with their actions.

And in case you were in any doubt:

> *"Some of the* **independent directors** *on AFM Boards did not provide the robust challenge we expect from them and*

appeared to **lack sufficient understanding** *of relevant fund rules."*

My translation: Some of the company directors are useless.

Let's summarise these points:

- You can't rely on them to tell the whole truth about fees, performance or objectives
- The more they charge, the worse they often are
- Their independent directors cannot be relied on to know what they're doing.

On 10 August 2023, the FCA published an update on this report in which they observe companies having "significantly improved their Assessment of Value processes."

I don't care about their processes; I want lower fees and better returns.

The update went on to say, "While we found firms had a better understanding for the need to justify fees, most remedial action did not involve cutting funds' fees."

Well, fancy that.

The FCA study looked into just 18 companies. These were selected to provide a representative sample of the entire community of 1,100 or so AFMs. Makes you wonder what they might have found had the review been comprehensive.

Of course, not all active managers are misleading, incompetent, lazy or greedy. But I have yet to see one that justifies what it charges year in, year out.

I was on the inside writing performance reports for over a decade in several different very large companies, so I think I know what I'm talking about.

They pay themselves very generously

The average total pay package for an "investment professional" in the UK is £216,591 according to Glassdoor.co.uk numbers in August 2023.

From what I've seen, this finding focuses on the senior managers, analysts, investment officers and so on. Also, it was very clearly indicated to me by the chief investment officer at a well-known company that the salaries for top management are much higher.

There's still the wage bill for all the support staff to account for. And all that money comes out of the company turnover before any profits are calculated.

IBISWorld found that the average profit margin for "fund management activities in the UK" was set to reach 21.8% in 2023. In other words, if a company has £10 million pounds of turnover each year, it gets to keep £2.18 million in profits.

All that money has to come from somewhere; specifically, it's being taken out of the money you hand over to them to invest.

Their business model

What they will do:

- Take your money and invest it
- Charge a fee which is taken directly out of your investment, every year, without fail.

What they won't do:

- Guarantee that you get a positive return
- Guarantee that any return you do get would be better than what you might have got if you'd put your money into a cheaper, passive fund.

What I think would be a much fairer business model:

1. They tell the truth in clear and simple language
2. Only have competent directors
3. Have an easy-to-understand and reasonable fee structure
4. Outperform cheaper passive funds each year AFTER FEES i.e., net performance
5. Deliver this outperformance consistently for a minimum of 10 years.

Remember what the FCA said in its report? Here's how it applies to the five points I've just listed:

1. Simple language: the FCA found that "many" of the firms it investigated are failing on this point
2. Directors: "some" of the directors are not meeting this, most basic, of standards according to the FCA
3. Simple and fair fees: this is frustratingly rare
4. Net performance: 57% of funds in the US underperformed the stock market in 2020
5. 10 years' outperformance: ha! – read the next chapter.

If there is an active management firm out there that can demonstrate that it fulfils all of my criteria and will continue to do so, please let me know who you are and I'll invest in you.

Bottom line

Even the financial watchdog is, shall we say, dismayed by some of the claims made by companies within the investment industry compared with what they actually deliver.

7 Active funds miss their targets

They do loads of research and analysis.
For which they charge really high fees.
They set their own targets.
...and miss them.

Here's the proof:

% of active funds underperforming their own benchmarks

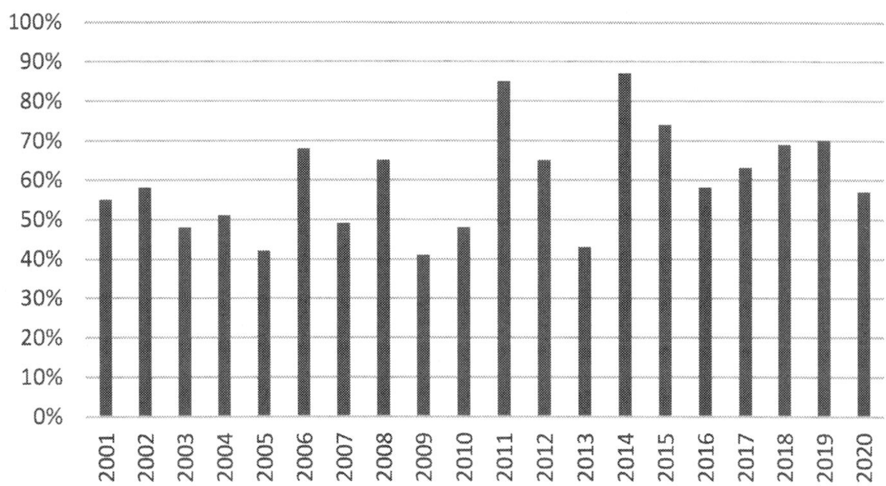

Source: S&P Dow Jones Indices LLC. Data as of 31 December 2020. https://www.spglobal.com/spdji/en/documents/spiva/spiva-us-year-end-2020.pdf

The US is the biggest investment market in the world, so I've taken data available on that market.

The chart above shows the percentage of active fund managers in the US that underperformed the targets (i.e., benchmarks) they set themselves, each year since 2001.

The best year for active fund managers was 2009 when 41% of firms failed to achieve their own benchmarks.

In other words, if you had a choice of 100 active management firms to choose from, 41 of them would fail to hit their own benchmarks. That's the best year in two decades.

In 14 out of the 20 years shown, more than half the fund managers covered by the data failed to hit the performance targets they set themselves. In nine of the 20 years, more than 60% of active fund managers missed their own targets.

What's more, it's going to be a different 50% or so firms each year that miss their own targets, so looking back at who has messed up in the past isn't going to help much.

What about bond funds?

The previous numbers focused on equity funds – those buying shares in companies.

According to US business magazine, *Forbes*, it's even worse with active bond funds (where the fund manager chooses different bonds to invest in instead of company shares): 90% of bond funds missed their benchmark targets in 2020

Cue the excuses

Here's the sort of conversation a fund manager might have with a disgruntled investor in the light of poor performance.

A common conversation?

Investor: Why did you do so badly?

Tied Advisor: It was a tumultuous year. No-one saw the pandemic/inflation/geopolitical challenges/recovery/summer coming, and that really sent share prices down very sharply.

Investor: But share prices rose very sharply after that. Why don't you capture those gains?

Tied Advisor: We did capture much of those gains, but the overall share prices haven't completely recovered yet.
Investor: Isn't that exactly the scenario in which your expertise should pay for itself? If I'd invested in a passive fund that just tracked the FTSE 100 (or something similar) then not only would the performance have been better, but I'd be paying much lower fees.
Tied Advisor: Yes, our fund has done badly in the short term, but we aim for long-term capital growth.
Investor: Hang on. Isn't that what the FCA quoted as being a nonsense excuse for poor performance?
Tied Advisor: I can't speak for other investment funds. What I can say is that if you were to withdraw your money now, you'd be locking in the losses and possibly exposing yourself to Capital Gains Tax charges.
Investor: But I haven't made much money with you, and my investments are in an ISA and a SIPP which are not subject to Capital Gains Tax.
Tied Advisor: Oh. That excuse normally works. OK, how about this one: It's not timing the market, it's time in the market that matters.

Rip-Off Tip-Off

An advisor friend of mine read this and said "This conversation is far too realistic!"

Investor: What does that mean in normal, everyday terms?
Tied Advisor: It means "Please don't withdraw your money from my fund"
Investor: Why not? What am I paying you for?
Tied Advisor: Our expertise and analysis. We have extensive research facilities and an investment philosophy that focuses on strategic asset allocation while also delivering best-in-class fund managers and an overlay of tactical asset flexibility.

Investor: What does that mean?
Tied Advisor: It means I know more about investments than you do.
Investor: If you know more about them, why is the performance so bad and the fees so high?
Tied Advisor: You've just answered your own question. If you knew more, you'd do what I do and never put your money into my funds.
Investor: What? You don't invest in your own firm's funds?
Tied Advisor: Hell no, they're dreadful. I put a tiny amount in so that when journalists ask, I can say "Oh yes, I put my money where my mouth is. I'm invested substantially in my fund."
Investor: What proportion of your wealth is in the fund?
Tied Advisor: I'm invested substantially in my fund.
Investor: 100% of my investments are with you. What percentage of yours are in your fund?
Tied Advisor: There are restrictions on how much I can put into the fund.
Investor: What percentage of your wealth is in your fund?
Tied Advisor: I'm invested substantially in my fund.
Investor: What am I really paying you for?
Tied Advisor: My two children. They're both in private education. Sebastian has just taken up lacrosse. Do you know how expensive those sticks are? And Cecilia-Juniper's polo pony won't feed itself.
Investor: I'm walking away now.
Tied Advisor: But wait. I've got a PowerPoint presentation with charts about how investors feel when investments up and go down.
Investor: Taxi!

It might sound like nonsense, but that conversation isn't a million miles from real conversations that go on every day between fund managers or tied advisors and their clients. The big difference between it and real-world conversations is that disgruntled investors are much more likely just to accept the fund manager's or the tied advisor's word.

Again, it's not just me who thinks this

Jayna Rana's article "Skin in the game: Managers can invest in their own fund…" for *This Is Money* in June 2020, wrote the following:

> "Those school fees, expensive house, fast cars and high-profile divorces don't pay for themselves."

Ahem, quite.

Bottom line

Their priority is them, not you.

8 1 in 3,333 beats the market

Using publicly available evidence, it would appear that 99.97% of active funds can't and won't beat the average market performance over the next five years. Here's how I reached that number.

The Investment Association, a UK industry body, recognises around 4,000 different UK funds (I have sifted through more than just these UK funds, and talk about them in Part Seven of this book). There are far more funds than there are investment firms or banks because each investment firm or bank is likely to run lots of different funds.

For example, a bank called, say, "Big Bank Corporation" might have a "Special Circumstances Fund," a "Global Equity Fund" and a "Balanced Growth Fund". That's one firm and three different funds.

I will, rather generously, assume that they are all honest and competent, despite the FCA's findings to the contrary.

By way of example, let's look at the 25 top-performing British funds in 2015 and see how many of those 25 did well in 2021 (the most recent data available to me at the time of writing).

In August 2015, TD Direct Investing released its "Best of British" list. *ThisIsMoney.co.uk* took this and produced the article "The 25 top-performing British fund managers over the last 10 years".

Here's the list with the average annual return over the preceding 10 years shown in the right-hand column:

	Fund	% return
1	SLI UK Smaller Companies Ret Acc	14.15
2	Old Mutual UK Smaller Companies Acc	13.91
3	CF Lindsell Train UK Equity Acc	12.04
4	Liontrust UK Smaller Companies Inc	11.97
5	Majedie UK Equity A Acc	11.21
6	Aberforth UK Small Companies Acc	11.06
7	Schroder UK Smaller Companies A Inc	10.60
8	Old Mutual UK Alpha R Acc	10.49
9	CF Woodford Equity Income	10.38
10	Kames Ethical Equity A Acc	9.34

11	JPM UK Smaller Companies A Acc	9.94
12	AXA Framlington UK Select Opps R Acc	9.84
13	Schroder UK Alpha Income A Inc	9.28
14	JOHCM UK Growth B GBP	9.01
15	SLI UK Ethical Ret Acc	9.00
16	Investec UK Special Situations A Inc Net	8.65
17	Artemis Income Inc	8.45
18	Liontrust Macro Equity Income	8.43
19	GAM UK Diversified Acc	8.43
20	Artemis UK Special Situations R Acc	8.35
21	Rathbone Income R Inc	8.07
22	Kames UK Equity E Acc	7.97
23	SLI UK Equity High Income Ret Inc	7.93
24	Rathbone Blue Chip Income And Growth	7.90
25	M&G Recovery A Acc	7.59

Now let's consider the article published by Citywire.com on 23 December 2021 entitled "Just 12 UK funds beat the market five years in a row...." By "beat the market" we are comparing the fund's performance to a major market index, such as the FTSE All-Share or the S&P 500.

Here are those 12:

Fund	2017 total return (%)	2018 total return (%)	2019 total return (%)	2020 total return (%)	2021 total return YTD to Oct (%)	Five year annualised total return to Oct 2021 (%)
MI Chelverton UK Equity Growth	33.3	-8.9	40.6	15.9	28.1	22.2
Allianz UK Listed Opportunities	15.5	-7.6	25.3	-5	25	11
Royal London UK Dividend Growth	16.6	-8.8	24.6	-3.9	20.7	10
Liontrust UK Growth	14.2	-6.1	19.9	-8.3	18.6	7.4
VT Sorbus Vector	16.5	-4.1	22.3	12.2	18.2	14.1

Royal London Sustainable Leaders	**15.8**	**-2**	**29.5**	**3.3**	**18**	**12.4**
GlobalAccess UK Opportunities	**14.6**	**-7.6**	**24**	**-9.6**	**17.9**	**7.6**
BMO Responsible UK Equity	**19.8**	**-6.9**	**23.2**	**-5.1**	**17.8**	**9.6**
Liontrust Special Situations	**16.8**	**-2.1**	**21.6**	**-1.2**	**17.6**	**10.8**
NFU Mutual UK Growth	**18.6**	**-8.9**	**24.1**	**-6.4**	**17**	**9**
ASI UK Mid-Cap Equity	**16.2**	**-8.4**	**39.6**	**4.7**	**16.3**	**13.6**
Dimensional UK Core Equity	**13.6**	**-9.1**	**20.2**	**-8.9**	**15.7**	**6.1**
FTSE All-Share	*13.1*	*-9.5*	*19.1*	*-9.8*	*15.6*	*5.6*

Not one fund made it onto both lists

How many funds appear in both lists i.e., how many funds delivered positive returns consistently over 15 years?

None. Not one. Nada. Zilch.

One or two investment *companies* appear on both lists, but what use is that to you? If your money is in the "Macro Equity" fund with Big Bank Corporation, you get no benefit at all from the "UK Equity" fund with Big Bank Corporation doing really well.

So out of the 4,000 or so funds, only 12 managed to beat the FTSE All-Share over the past five years. And not one of them was a top performer back in 2015.

The impossible challenge

You are left with the challenge of finding the 12 out of 4,000 funds that will beat the FTSE All-Share Index over the next five years. And no amount of past data will help you with this unlucky dip.

I'll make it easier for you. I'll double it from 12 to 24. Heck, let's go crazy: I'll pretend that 40 funds will do well. That gives you a

40 in 4,000 chance or 1% (1 in 100) chance of picking an active fund that beats the market.

It happens everywhere

And, just to be clear, this awful long-term performance compared to "passive" funds isn't unique to the UK or US. It's universal.

In 2019, the European Securities and Markets Authority (ESMA) issued its Report on Trends, Risks and Vulnerabilities of investment funds that you and I can invest in across the European Union.

This noted that "active equity [funds] have underperformed on average, in net terms, passive and ETF equity [funds] as well as their prospectus benchmarks."

You are faced with literally thousands of funds with complicated names (64,000 if you're looking at the data collection website, Morningstar).

You have a less-than 1% chance of choosing one that will beat the average market performance over five- to 10-years.

You have no valuable data to go by.

Good luck!

Either way, the fees will kill you

For the heck of it, let's assume you've done it. You've beaten the odds and chosen an active fund that will outperform the FTSE All-Share Index over the next five years.

In fact, let's assume you've chosen an active fund that will be one of the top 25 performers over the next 10 years. It'll do really well, matching the average performance of the top 25 performers shown above from 2005 to 2015. That's an annual return of 9.8%.

Wow, go you! Great yeah?

Nope.

This sentence in the *ThisIsMoney.co.uk* article caught my eye:

> "The top 25 beat the FTSE All-Share by a significant margin, the study found, producing an average return per annum of 9.8% over the decade against 7.1% for the FTSE."

The first thing that struck me when I read the 9.8% average annual return was "what was the average annual return after fees?" i.e., what returns will you, the investor, actually receive?

Brace yourself, the next chapter heaps more misery on the investor who has money with an active fund.

Bottom line

Try as they might, almost every manager of active funds can't consistently deliver better returns AFTER FEES than passive funds.

9

I save 90% on fees

Or, to put it another way, the Ongoing Charges Figure (OCF) that I pay, is ***at least*** 10-times cheaper than the average OCF of an active fund. It's even cheaper than the average OCF of a passive fund.

According to the FCA:
Active funds average OCF: **0.89%**
Passive funds average OCF: **0.15%**
My portfolios weighted OCF: from **0.06% to 0.08%**

Rip-Off Tip-Off

In case you're wondering, the term "weighted" when referring to the Ongoing Charges Figure (OCF) allows for how much you get charged for each investment in your portfolio. For example, assume you have £1,000 in a global bonds fund and it charges 0.3%, that will cost 0.3% x £1,000 = £30. Also assume you have £2,000 in a global shares fund that charges 0.1%, which will cost 0.1% x £2,000 = £20. The total weighted OCF is £30 + £20 = £50. And relax.

Let's look at how I reached those numbers.

Small numbers make a massive difference

The fee numbers sound small. That's how active funds can convince people to pay them.

If a firm charges you 1% a year, then that's 1% of the total investment you place with them. It's also 1% of the total investment you have with them every single year thereafter.

If they're aiming to grow investments by 3% a year, one third of that growth goes into their pockets.

And that's assuming they can even hit their own targets which, as we've seen, virtually none of them can over a sustained period of time.

It also doesn't accurately reflect the total fees that they charge (remember Posh Investments back in Chapter 4?)

Active fund fees charge an average 0.89%

According to the FCA (the investment industry watchdog), fees charged by active fund managers have been coming down over recent years. I should jolly well hope so. They're still far higher than those charged by passive funds.

But even so, I'm not convinced that 0.89% reflects what you and I, ordinarly investors, are charged by active fund managers. I think it's a good chunk higher than that. Nevertheless, let's stick with the FCA's number, it makes for grim enough results.

Here's what the FCA said in its Investment management data – Annual Report 2020/21:

> "Average ongoing fees for UK-domiciled active funds have declined from 1.08% of AUM [assets under management] per year in 2015, to reach 1.0% in 2018 and then 0.89% in 2020."

And that's just the "average" ongoing fees. It doesn't allow for all the fees/charges/costs that you, the investor, have to pay though.

Others fees/charges include transaction fees (buying and selling shares), underlying manager fees (other fund managers who might get an allocation from the fund manager that you put your money with) and a host of others.

Nevertheless, let's take that average of 0.89%. If you have £10,000 invested in year 1, you'd lose £89 of it at the end of that year in the fees charged just by the fund.

Passive funds charge an average 0.15%

In the same article, the FCA went on to describe the fees charged by passive funds:

> "Average ongoing fees for UK-domiciled passive funds have declined from 0.29% of AUM per year in 2015, to reach 0.25% in 2018 and then 0.15% in 2020."

The funds in my portfolios charge fees of between 0.05% and 0.08%

The portfolios I set up in Part 7 incur weighted OCFs of just 0.05%-0.08%. The variation depends on how much the investment portfolio is, and what level of risk I find to be appropriate from my risk assessment questionnaire in Chapter 16.

If you want to see the working behind this, go to "I save 90% in fees" in the Appendix.

Let's think about the saving for a moment. Active fund managers (i.e., most banks and investment companies), want to charge you 0.89% on average. I have similar mixture of shares and bonds for just 0.08% or less.

Rip-Off Tip-Off

They are charging more than 10-times what I consider to be a fair price.
Rip-off? You decide.

That small number makes a huge difference

In my portfolios, the "ongoing charge" on my £10,000 investment would be £8 at the most. £89 vs. £8 might not sound like much, but it's compounded year after year.

Take a spectacularly unusual active fund with a gross return of 9.8%. Remove the 0.89% total fees from that to determine the net return that you'll actually receive, namely 8.91% a year, every year. That's still very good (if nigh on impossible to find according to the statistics).

The much more likely and easier-to-find passive equivalent would be 7.1% gross return - 0.15% fee = 6.95% average annual net return.

Compounding – a quick explanation of how it works

Compounding boils down to leaving any growth or profit you have made in the investment; don't take anything out, just let it do its thing.

It's best explained by using an example.

Start by investing £10,000 which you leave for 10 years at a 10% rate of return.

(Incidentally, 10% is a massive annual return and incredibly unlikely, but it makes the hypothetical example easy to follow.)

Not compounded, you'll end up with £20,000.
Compounded, you'll end up with £25,937

Let's look at how that happens.

Not compounded

If you start with £10,000 and get a 10% return that does not compound, then you get £1,000 each year. That will leave you with a total of £20,000 at the end of 10 years.

Original capital of £10,000 plus £10,000 (£1,000 a year for 10 years) = £20,000.

Compounded

By contrast, if you get a 10% return that does compound, then the 10% increase is applied to the total amount at the end of each year, not just the original £10,000, as follows:

End of year 1: £10,000 + 10% (£1,000) = £11,000
End of year 2: £11,000 + 10% (£1,100) =£12,100
End of year 3: £12,100 + 10% (£1,210) = £13,310
End of year 4: £13,310 + 10% (£1,331) = £14,641
End of year 5: £14,641 + 10% (£1,464) = £16,105
End of year 6: £16,105 + 10% (£1,611) = £17,716
End of year 7: £17,716 + 10% (£1,772) = £19,487
End of year 8: £19,487 + 10% (£1,949) = £21,436
End of year 9: £21,436 + 10% (£2,144) = £23,579
End of year 10: £23,579 + 10% (£2,358) = £25,937

Passive funds don't exactly match what they track

A passive fund or "tracker" follows the ups and downs of the overall market. It does that by copying the performance of an index that represents the overall market. As mentioned, two examples of such indices are the S&P 500 in the US and the FTSE All-Share in the UK.

Try as it might, a tracker can never exactly match what the index does. This difference between the target benchmark index (e.g., the FTSE All-Share) and the tracker fund or passive fund is referred to as the tracking error.

According to that same report by the FCA:

> "In the 12 months to April 2021, 95.3% of AUM [assets under management] UK-domiciled passive funds tracked their benchmarks to within 75 basis points, up from 92.5% in the 12 months to April 2020, a marginal improvement in tracking performance despite heightened market volatility in the first quarter of 2020."

What this means is that the vast majority (95.3%) of UK passive funds were within 0.75 of a percentage point of the index (e.g., FTSE 100) or commodity (e.g., gold price) that they were tracking.

For example, if the FTSE All-Share rose (or fell) by 5%, then passive funds rose (or fell) by between 4.25% and 5.75%.

Why the tracking error matters

Let's assume the worst-case scenario for the passive fund and assume that it always underperforms its target benchmark by 0.75 of a percentage point. That's an unfair misrepresentation of what passive funds actually do, but I'm doing this to demonstrate how bad active funds strike me as being compared to passive funds.

This "worst case" brings the passive fund's performance down from 6.85% to 6.10%. Let's round it down to 6.0% for simplicity and to really stack the odds in favour of active funds.

Realistic active fund returns

Now we need a fair representation of what performance or returns an average active fund will deliver.

As we've seen, there's a ton of evidence showing that the vast majority of active funds underperform passive funds over time. A quick search on the Internet will confirm this if you want to check for yourself.

The question is, what is a representative level of underperformance? 1%-a-year worse, 20%? More?

It varies hugely so I'm going to provide a range of performance levels by active funds, including two that outperform passive funds. Unlikely, but possible.

Remember, the gross returns are what most active funds report. But these are irrelevant because they don't allow for the fees the fund manager charges.

What you really need to know is the net returns – what you get after the fund manager has taken its fees. That applies to both passive (which tend to be more transparent about performance) and active fund managers.

The following chart draws on the numbers from the FCA to show:

- The returns AFTER FEES of a passive fund that's at the lower range of passive fund performance and tracking
- A range of returns AFTER FEES of active funds
- All returns are compounded.

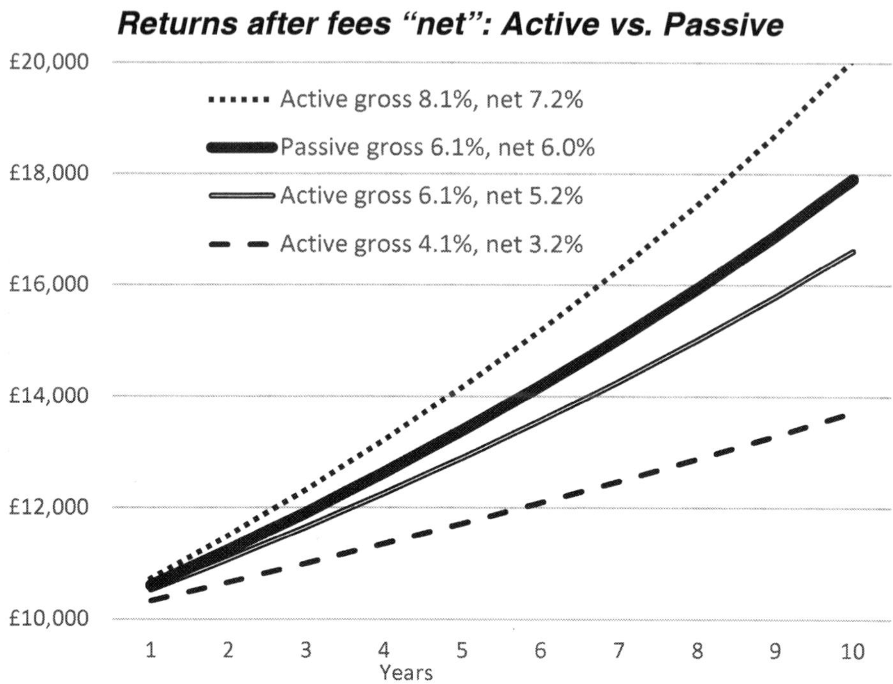

This chart shows very roughly how a £10,000 investment might grow over 10 years at different annual rates of return. The returns are compounded i.e., for the entire 10-year period, all profits are reinvested as they arrive and no money is withdrawn.

What the lines in the chart mean

The green line - the passive fund

The green line shows an annual return, after fees, of 6.0% each year for 10 years.

How I got 6.0%:

1. I started with the 7.1% annualised return of the FTSE All Share Index (see end of Chapter 8)
2. I then whacked an exaggerated 0.75% off that to account for a maximum and always negative tracking error. This is extremely unlikely, but I want to give active funds every possible advantage.
3. I then took a further 0.15% off that for the heck of it.

The other lines - the active funds

The other lines show how an active fund would have performaned if:

1. Dots - It had outperformed the passive fund by 2% before fees
2. Dashes - It had matched the passive fund before fees
3. Dots and Dashes - It had underperformed the passive fund by 2% before fees.

You have a 1 in 3,333 chance of finding an active fund that will deliver this performance over just five years according to the research conducted by information publishing group, CityWire. Over 10 years, it's going to be even more unlikely that you'll find an outperforming active fund.

Even with all these disadvantages, the passive fund still outperforms the vast majority of active funds after fees.

Rip-Off Tip-Off

You are seven-times more likely to be born with 11 fingers or toes than have an active fund that outperforms a passive one after fees.

Historic numbers

The next chart shows how these numbers might have worked if you'd had a passive fund over the past 10 years.

Remember that a pitiful 12 out of 40,000 active funds (or 1 in every 3,333) in the UK managed to beat passive funds over 10 years.

That's a 99.97% chance that you won't find an active fund that will perform better than a passive fund over 10 years (even though the active fund probably charges six-times as much).

Major indicies' performance over the past 10 years

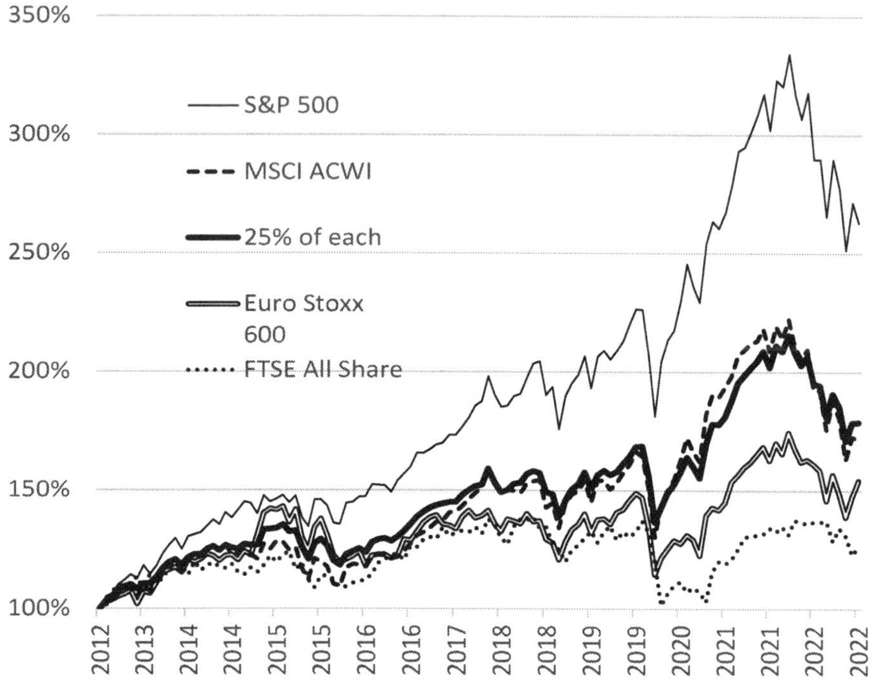

Source: Refinitiv/LSEG, December 2022

IMPORTANT: You must remember that these numbers are historic and, as such, cannot and must not be used as an indication of what will happen in the future.

The chart shows what £10,000 might have returned if it had been invested in passive funds tracking stock markets in the US, UK, eurozone and the world.

Don't put all your eggs in one basket

It looks as though the US shares market, represented by the S&P 500, would be the best bet. If you had invested in November 2012 then the S&P 500 would indeed have grown the most.

However, if you had started your investment in November 2021, the S&P 500 would have been the worst performing of the four, dropping by 22% until August 2022. By contrast, the FTSE All-

Share would have dropped by only 6% over much the same period.

I know that it's impossible to predict how shares in the UK, US, Europe or anywhere else are going to perform. So why not spread the £10,000 across all four of the indices in the chart?

The thick black line represents how that average would have performed.

It shows a total return of 79% over the full 10-year period. Using a compound calculation, that equates to 6% a year "annualised" return, which is roughly what we expected from the FCA's own numbers.

Do it more cheaply

But if I'm putting money into four different passive funds tracking four different indices, I'd have to pay four different sets of fees.

Why not just put money into a passive fund that tracks the global index (in this case, the MSCI ACWI)? That way I'll get the diversification but for lower fees.

Annualised returns demystified

Annualised return is effectively another way of saying "compound growth rate".

By leaving all the money in the investment, the 6% of annual growth applies to the entire investment held over the previous 12 months, not just the amount you initially invested.

At the end of the first year, 6% would be paid on the total investment. 6% of £10,000 is £600 bringing the total to £10,600.

So, the second year would begin with £10,600.
At the end of the second year, there'd be another 6% added to the entire investment; the 6% is paid on £10,600. That's an

additional £636 pounds. £10,600 + £636 = £11,236 at the end of year two.

It works like this, year after year, as follows:

End of year 1: £10,000 plus 6% (£600) = £10,600
End of year 2: £10,600 plus 6% (£636) = £11,236
End of year 3: £11,236 plus 6% (£674) = £11,910
End of year 4: £11,910 plus 6% (£715) = £12,625
End of year 5: £12,625 plus 6% (£757) = £13,382
End of year 6: £13,382 plus 6% (£803) = £14,185
End of year 7: £14,185 plus 6% (£851) = £15,036
End of year 8: £15,036 plus 6% (£902) = £15,938
End of year 9: £15,938 plus 6% (£956) = £16,895
End of year 10: £16,895 plus 6% (£1,014) = £17,908

After 10 years of 6% annualised compound growth, the investment would have grown by a total of 79% i.e., £7,908 on top of the original £10,000 invested.

Be patient

It's essential to allow the investment time to do its thing. If we'd taken the money out in February 2020 when Covid-19 was hitting and everything was looking horribly bleak, the return would have totalled just 36%. Less than two years later in November 2021, the total return would have been 116%.

My preferred investment approach is to put money in the right selection of investments that track the markets and don't charge unfair fees, then forget about it for at least a year.

There's no way of accurately predicting what the markets are going to do next, so don't even try. Just leave your money where it is and get on with your life.

The low-cost funds that I like

I prefer passive funds; funds which copy the performance of an index (such as the FTSE 100) or another asset (such as gold).

These cost far less because the process is automated. There are no people being paid to research and analyse companies and markets in a (largely forlorn) attempt to deliver higher returns than the market average.

I've identified over 100 passive funds that are low-cost and which allow me to build appropriate portfolios for a fraction of what most banks and investment companies want to charge.

Before I share those with you, we need to take a few steps to make sure that investing is the right thing to do.

Bottom line

Why pay far more than you need to?

PART THREE

The Foundations

10 Current situation and aspirations

Here's a quick outline of what I believe anyone should seriously consider doing before investing:

- Write down your financial aspirations
- Assess your financial situation
- Clear any "bad" debt
- Check your state pension
- Set up a cash buffer
- Complete a risk-appetite assessment
- Set up an appropriate investment portfolio
- Get on with your life and leave the investments to do their thing.

Let's look at these in turn over the next few chapters.

Write down your goals and aspirations

These don't have to be massively ambitious. It might be that you want to be able to put a deposit down on a property, pay for education, cover later-life health costs, pass on some inheritance, set up a decent retirement fund or fulfil a host of other achievable goals.

Until you write them down, it'll be harder to create a simple plan on how to get there and turn them into reality.

Assess your current financial situation

This is possibly the most important step you need to take to improve your financial future.

It's a simple thing to do and yet you might be daunted at the prospect. Don't be. It takes a bit of time and effort, but it's simple and 100% worthwhile.

Make a list of:

Your income/ benefits/ salary/ rental income, etc.

Your outgoings/ expenses/ mortgage payments/ food/ insurance/ MOT, etc.

Your cash/ investments/ pensions/ Individual Savings Accounts (ISAs)/Self-Invested Personal Pensions (SIPPs), etc.

You'll find ready-made lists available to download for free on these impartial, government-funded websites:

- MoneyAndPensionsService.org.uk
- CitizensAdvice.org.uk

These sites consider a broad financial remit including money troubles, benefits and family care. They contain some good articles on pensions and savings.

If you ever need an entirely neutral, reliable source of information, I'd recommend them. They can even offer free counselling and advice for people struggling with finances.

What your list tells you

Take the time to dig out your bank and credit card statements, investment statements and other information that you need to be as comprehensive as possible.

When you've completed the spreadsheet, you'll:

- Know what your current financial situation really is
- Be able to prioritise what to do next
- Be able to plan how to achieve the financial goals that you want
- Begin to eliminate the worry and stress related to bills, money and investing.

Getting professional, independent advice

This might be a good point at which to obtain financial advice. As covered in chapter 5, my preference would be to seek out an IFA who covers the "whole-of-market," rather than a tied advisor who can only offer what his or her company wants to sell. Expect to pay around £1,500 for their advice.

There are some delightful and very decent tied advisors, but that's irrelevant to me because they can only offer a restricted range of investments. And these investments are much more likely to carry higher charges. For me, tied agents are a non-starter.

As a reminder, companies or banks with tied advisors will come up with various reasons why these salaried advisors are better than the independent ones. I don't buy this for these simple reasons:

1. All advisors are obliged by law to give the most appropriate advice for the client. So, unless they're breaking the law, it's irrelevant if they're salaried or not.

2. Whole-of-market IFAs have a broader range of investments from which to choose and are not targeted to sell specific funds. Very often, investment houses and banks will have between three and seven investment portfolios. That makes it cost-efficient for them to run, but is any one of those right for my unique circumstances?

3. Whole-of-market IFAs can tailor investments to my particular circumstances if I want them to. (I don't happen to use them because I know what I'm doing.) But, if I were to choose an IFA, I would value their ability to tailor investments around my circumstances.

Clear any "bad" debt

In broad terms, I consider the mortgage on your home to be a "good" debt. I consider most other debt to be bad.

Why is good debt good?

A mortgage can provide somewhere to live and a form of long-term investment. Depending on your circumstances, it can make sense to maintain payments and not pay the mortgage off early.

As always, this is just a general rule of thumb; your specific circumstances will determine the precise action you should take.

Avoid this big mistake

Some people have both savings and "bad" debt. That can be a big and expensive mistake.

Here's why.

These debts charge high interest, usually far more than you're going to earn through savings.

Don't kid yourself that it's nice to have savings when you also have the sort of debts that I've listed. It's an expensive mistake.

Hypothetical example of savings that cost you money

You might be holding £1,000 of debt on one hand which charges an average of, say, 15% a year (though it's probably more—I was paying 29.8% on my credit card until I moved it to a cheaper loan and paid that off).

Meanwhile, the £1,000 in savings that you hold probably pays less than 5%.

In other words, you're maybe earning £50 a year BEFORE TAX on your savings and paying £150 a year in interest payments on your credit card. That nice-to-have-savings feeling is costing you £100 a year from your after-tax earnings.

In essence, you're subsidising the credit companies. **Don't fall for it.** Clear that debt.

If you can't pay them all off, consider:

- Moving the ones charging the highest interest rates to lower-interest rate options
- Paying off the most expensive ones as quickly as possible
- Using the free resources mentioned below to help you get your debt under control.

A note about credit cards

The culture of buying on credit is great for the credit card companies. They make between 2% and 5% on each purchase and then a further fee that can be as high as 30% for money not repaid within 30 days.

Some argue that credit cards can be useful and they might be right. If you're good at juggling low-cost or zero-interest credit cards, keep the end-of-month balance clear, and can justify the up-front fees for such cards, then good luck to you.

I want a simple life in which I don't spend any more time than absolutely necessary thinking about money, debt or investments. Hence I don't have any debt at all.

If you absolutely must have a credit card then I think Jasmine Birtles (of MoneyMagpie.com) has a good approach; have one credit card for emergencies on which you've cleared the balance. Put it into a watertight plastic bag, put the bag into a small plastic box filled with water and put the sealed box in your freezer.

If you really need the card, you can defrost the card overnight, giving you time to think about whether you really need whatever it is you were thinking of buying. If you microwave the block of ice containing the card, you'll destroy the card. This way, you absolutely have to wait at least one day before using it.

Free, impartial advice on debt

If you're unsure about your debt situation, experiencing problems paying your bills, drowning in debt or just getting stressed about debt, here are four organisations you can go to for genuine, free advice and guidance:

- Money Helper (formerly Money Advice Service) - www.moneyhelper.org.uk
- National Debt Line—www.nationaldebtline.org
- Citizens Advice Bureau—www.citizensadvice.org.uk/debt-and-money/
- Step Change— www.stepchange.org

Rip-Off Tip-Off

Whatever you do, DO NOT go to any "loan consolidators" or anyone else who advertises on TV or radio, or in magazines. If they can afford to advertise then they're getting the money to do so by ripping people off.

Bottom line

Don't skip this stage.

11 Your state pension

If you're living in the UK, the chances are that you'll be entitled to a state pension. At the time of writing in 2023, the state pension provides up to £203.85 per week. That might not sound like much, but don't dismiss it: it's actually very valuable.

State pension vs salary

To take home £200 a week from a salary, you'd need to be earning a gross annual salary of around £10,600. Imagine someone offering you a £10,600 annual pay rise right now in return for which you just have to stay alive. Would you refuse?

State pension vs annuity

The value of the state pension is even more striking when you compare it to an annuity, i.e., a financial product that pays you an amount each year depending on such factors as:

- How much money you commit upfront to buy the annuity
- How long you want the annuity to last
- If it will rise with inflation i.e., if it's "index-linked"

I like to think of the state pension as an annuity which is index-linked and indefinite - it only stops paying once I'm no longer around to collect it.

Insurance and investment companies will sell annuities. But they do it to make a profit. That means that you would have to pay a heart-stoppingly hefty sum to get an annuity that would pay £180 a week, rise with inflation, and continue until death do you part.

How hefty? Perhaps around £200,000 for a 55-year-old or maybe less if you're older.

Yep, from the conversations I've had with financial advisors, an upfront payment in the very approximate ballpark of £200,000 could be required to generate the equivalent of the UK state pension. Which makes the state pension one heck of a gift horse.

Rip-Off Tip-Off

You might find advisors who offer to arrange an annuity "for free". Don't be fooled, it ain't. The commission that you'll pay indirectly can be nothing short of outrageous.

Frightening data

According to the Office for National Statistics dataset *Pension Wealth: Wealth in Great Britain*, the average pension pot of UK individuals at the age of 55 is, wait for it, just £75,500.

This tells us many things, including:

- The majority of people have nowhere near enough for retirement
- The state pension is massively important to most people.

Check your state pension

The UK government website https://www.gov.uk/check-state-pension provides useful and easy-to-follow steps on:

- How much pension you're entitled to
- When you can retire
- How to increase your state pension entitlement

Visit that website and follow the instructions to set up an account (it's fiddly but worth it).

Once you have an account, you'll be able to find out how much your state pension is likely to be at retirement. The figure will depend on a number of factors, most important of which could be the National Insurance (NI) contributions you've made to date. Currently, you need to have made 35 years of NI contributions to receive a full state pension.

If your state pension pot is not on target to hit full value, then seriously consider making some extra contributions to boost it. It's one of the best-value pensions in my opinion.

HOWEVER, you should be aware that the government is pushing back the retirement age, so you might not be entitled to collect a state pension until you're 67.

The reason is obvious. As people live longer, the cost of pensions is proving too much for the public purse. Something has to give, and, with most folk reluctant to pay more tax or NI contributions, the cost of pensions is being managed by postponing the date on which the payments can kick in.

Nevertheless, I keep a close eye on my NI contributions to make sure that I'll be entitled to the full state pension. For me, it's too good an offer to miss out on.

Bottom line

The UK state pension won't be enough to live on, but it can make a massive difference.

12 Cash buffer

This slightly irritating statement is true: "Only invest money you can afford to lose. Investments can go down as well as up. You might get back less than you invested."

In other words, make sure you're financially set up to be able to cope with the unexpected before you invest.

Why you need a buffer

Being unprepared for the unexpected is one of the biggest failings of folk in the UK.

For how long would you be able to manage financially if you suddenly lost your job or your ability to earn money? For most people, the answer is probably around three months. That's a very vulnerable position.

The following are the sorts of things that life throws at us all at some point or another:

- Unemployment
- Illness/ accident
- New washing machine
- House maintenance issues
- Car breakdown
- Divorce

The emotional pressure of these events is enough to deal with, let alone having the additional stress of managing the financial implications.

When you encounter one of these events, your normal cash flow is bound to be disrupted. As a result, you'll probably find yourself needing some money to tide you over until things settle down.

Rip-Off Tip-Off

One of the trustworthy financial advisors I spoke to about this said that, while the rule of thumb among advisors is to have five years' worth of cash buffer, he reckons one to two years is more realistic. For me, even that's too much, but I'm not an advisor. Suffice to say that I want to be in a position not to have to sell my investments to pay for something that comes up.

If you don't have a cash buffer, you'll end up having to dip into your investments or, worse still, borrow money. Selling investments at short notice is expensive because:

- You'll get a poor price for whatever you're selling
- You'll incur trading costs
- You may also incur transfer/extraction costs.

As a consequence, that £5,000 which you need immediately will actually cost you more like £5,500 or more, AND it will take you months to rectify the damage done to your investments.

Don't let that happen to you.

Set up that cash buffer. You'll be glad you did, if only for the fact that it massively reduces stress and worry.

After you've cleared your bad debt, work out how much your monthly outgoings are and start saving three to six months' worth of cash; that's the sort of amount I prefer to use, but you may choose to use more.

How much do you need?

Look back over your expenditure for the past six months. Your bank balance should provide you with most of the information you need.

Make sure you allow for things that you pay for annually but which did not fall during that six-month period (e.g., annual insurance, school fees, holidays, Christmas, council tax and so on).

Work out how much your expenditure is over that period. That's a good target to have as a cash buffer.

With a cash buffer in place, I'm much less likely to fret about the ups and downs of my investments. Similarly, if something bad happens, I'm in a position to pay for emergency healthcare or to cover my expenses after being made redundant.

Example with numbers

The median weekly pay for full-time employees was £640 in April 2022, according to the Office for National Statistics. That equates to about £33,280 a year.

There is massive variation on this, though, depending on age, gender and location. And that's before we think about the different areas of work that you might be engaged in.

A ballpark figure for the take-home pay (after tax and NI) from £33,280 is £26,650 in the 2023-2024 tax year.

To keep it simple, I'm going to think of six months' worth of this as £12,000. So, when I talk about the cash buffer, I'm going to use £12,000 as the figure.

Your figure is likely to be different from this but it's a good number to use by way of example.

What do you do with that money?

The point of the cash buffer isn't to make money, but to have readily available cash in the case of an emergency.

The simplest way of doing this is to put the cash buffer into a savings account.

The rate of interest is probably not going to be very good. In all likelihood, it'll be lower than inflation (the rate at which prices for goods and services rise).

The consequence of this is that, even though the total number of £12,000 will remain largely unchanged, what it can buy over time will fall.

But that doesn't matter because my priority is to have cash readily available. If I were particularly worried about inflation, I'd just add another 15 days' worth of cash to the total, making it a six-and-half-month buffer.

The next step is to forget about it. It's there doing its job of being my cash backup should I need it. That allows me to sleep easy, and that's really what this book is all about: peace of mind.

Use the UK government's guarantee

I'd make sure that the bank with which I'm placing the buffer is covered by the Financial Services Compensation Scheme (FSCS) (for more information, visit fscs.org.uk).

That way, should the bank I've put the money with go bust a la Northern Rock, I'd get my money paid back to me by the government up to a total of £85,000 (at the time of writing).

There is one caveat to add to this, and it's important. The FSCS guarantee of £85,000 applies as a total of all your holdings under a banking licence, which can include more than one company as you and I see them.

By way of example, Clydesdale Bank, Virgin Money and Yorkshire Bank are all covered by the same banking licence, so the £85,000 FSCS guarantee includes everything I might hold across all three in total.

The Bank of England provides a list of banking companies according to their respective banking licences. This is where I found the latest version when writing the book: https://www.bankofengland.co.uk/-/media/boe/files/prudential-regulation/authorisations/which-firms-does-the-pra-regulate/2022/list-of-banking-brands-july-2022.pdf

If I were lucky enough to have £85,000 across all of them, then I'd be looking for a banking group covered by a different banking licence in which to place anything over the £85,000.

All that said, I'd be surprised if too many people would need an £85,000 cash buffer!

Bottom line

IFAs advise people to have a cash buffer in place before investing. It makes sense. Do it.

13 What are you investing for?

There are dozens of reasons why you might be investing. I'm not going to go into all of them because it really all boils down to one of two scenarios, the first of which leads to the second:

- To build up a nest egg i.e., investments that grow in value
- To generate income from an existing nest egg i.e., investments that provide an income.

Other reasons for investing are beyond the scope of this book.

Below are some of the things that you might be hoping to achieve (you can add plenty of your own aspirations and goals to these lists).

Nest egg goals:

- Deposit for a house or apartment
- University fees for your children or grandchildren
- A second/ holiday home
- To provide for retirement living expenses
- To be able to retire early
- Don't really know yet, but feel you ought to be setting money aside (you're right, you should).

Income-generating goals:

- Living expenses during retirement
- Paying for later-life care needs
- Travelling
- Supporting good causes

In this book, I focus on investing for capital growth i.e., nest egg goals. I'll add more information about income-generating goals on the website that goes with the book.

If you are at a stage where you need to take an income from your investments, you probably need independent financial advice that will address your unique circumstances.

Whatever you're investing for, you'll need to choose investments that are designed to meet the level of risk that's appropriate for you.

So, let's talk about risk.

Bottom line

It's much more exciting and "real" if you have a clear picture of what you'll be using the invested money for.

PART FOUR

Risk Made Simple

14 Risk is good if used properly

Risk is a part of investing just as much as it is a part of life. If you never risk leaving the house then you might avoid getting rained on or being hit by a bus, but you'd also never hear the birds singing or be able to get work, buy food, meet friends and so on.

I'll show you how to find out the right level of risk for you with my risk assessment questionnaire in chapter 16.

For now, the point I'm making here is that risk, in itself, isn't a bad thing. Too much or, indeed, too little risk is the problem.

You cannot completely avoid risk

Everything to do with savings and investment carries risk of some sort. Don't try to avoid it completely, it's not possible.
For example, keeping cash under the mattress carries the risk that it will lose spending-power value due to inflation. That's aside from the possibility of it being siphoned away by your teenage relative or eaten by your pet hamster.

That's why it's essential, before investing, to:

1. Clear your bad debt
2. Set up a cash buffer
3. Consider the appropriate level of risk in your investments.

We've dealt with 1 and 2, so let's look at 3 because it will have a big influence on your choice of investments.

Using the right money

From now on, you need to be dealing with money that, were you to lose it, you wouldn't be ruined or pushed into financial trouble.

So, don't use borrowed money for these investments, nor your cash buffer and heed my earlier note about credit cards. Break these rules and you're leaving yourself vulnerable to unforeseen circumstances.

Inflation erodes the value of cash

Inflation i.e., the rate at which prices are rising, has become a very hot topic of late. After years of incredibly low inflation (under 2% a year), the rate has shot up as a result of Covid-19, Russia invading Ukraine, etc.

The higher inflation is, the less your money will buy in one year's time. At 2%, the average basket of goods and services costing £100 this year would cost £102 next year. At an inflation rate of

10%, rather than needing £102 next year to buy the same basket of goods, you'd need £110.

Or, to put it another way albeit in simplified terms, at an inflation rate of 10%, £100 this year is worth roughly £90 next year.

The consequence is that any cash you hold is losing value in terms of what you can purchase with it. The higher the rate of inflation, the faster it loses this purchasing power.

That's not to say that holding cash is bad: it's not. I always have some cash in my portfolio for reasons that I'll cover in Part Five – Different types of investment or "asset classes".

But you must recognise that by choosing to hold cash, you HAVE made an investment decision, you HAVE NOT avoided risk. You must recognise this reality if you want to keep lots of money as cash rather than investing it.

Risk and reward

Every fund that you and I can invest in, active or passive, is required by law to show its "risk and reward profile." Here's an example:

← Potentially lower reward				Potentially higher reward →		
← Lower risk					Higher risk →	
1	2	3	4	5	6	7

In this example, the risk-reward rating is "4", which is "medium" risk.

What official risk ratings mean

Unfortunately, in my opinion, this official definition of "risk" is vague and a bit useless for the ordinary investor.

It considers a lot of technical risk-related stuff that does carry legitimate value. For example, how much the price of the investment in question moves up and down ("volatility"), how easy/difficult it is to sell the investment and get your cash out quickly ("liquidity"), how likely the other party is to run off with your money or go bust ("counterparty risk") and so on.

The higher the potential return, the higher the risk

If there's a higher potential return (it's never guaranteed in the real world), then there is a higher risk of you losing your some or all of your money.

The more important to you that your money is, or the sooner you're going to need it, the less risk you should be taking with it.

Remember Northern Rock and those Icelandic banks that went bust? They were paying higher interest rates to customers with savings accounts than any other banks were.

They were able to do it because they were taking higher risks with customers' money. After a few years, that level of risk caught up with them and they went bust.

Customers did eventually get their money back thanks to government reimbursements (hence the importance and value of the £85,000 Financial Services Compensation Scheme (FSCS) see Glossary and Index for references in this book).

In the case of the Icelandic banks, the customers' money was not government-guaranteed and was, in effect, repaid by Icelandic tax payers.

Why these risk-reward number ratings are a bit useless

While their risk rating provides some relevant information, they are, in truth, imprecise.

For example, several risk-rated portfolios I studied across lots of companies all earned a "4" on this risk-rating measurement.

However, they included what the providers themselves described as lower-, medium- and higher-risk portfolios.

In more technical terms, the risk-ratings are also a bit useless because they're based on historical data. We're all tired of hearing "past performance is not an indication of future performance, trousers may go down as well as up, your house may be at risk if you leave your teenage son alone in it for the weekend, etc." Prices of bonds, shares, funds, gold, Uncle Tom Cobley and all, went all over the place during the Covid-19 pandemic. The risk ratings were naff-all use then.

What's more, the risk-rating number doesn't tell you if the fund manager is going deliver shoddy performance which, as we've seen, almost all active funds will.

Simple examples of low- and high-risk investments

I'm going to lead you through a simple, step-by-step guide to what "risk" means in terms of investment choices. This is meant as a rough indication rather than a technically specific guide.

There are plenty of places where you can get technical info like this, for example at www.Investopedia.com.

How to understand the following chart

The green line represents US government bonds (see below for explanation of what shares and bonds are).

The blue line represents the overall value of the largest 500 US companies in which you can buy shares.

The numbers have been adjusted to show how the shares and bonds rose and fell from the year 2000. Think of the numbers on the vertical axis as percentages; in 2009, bonds were up 50% relative to their starting value in the year 2000, while shares were down 50%.

US government bonds are lower risk. This can be seen because the up and down movements are less extreme, especially from 2017 onwards.

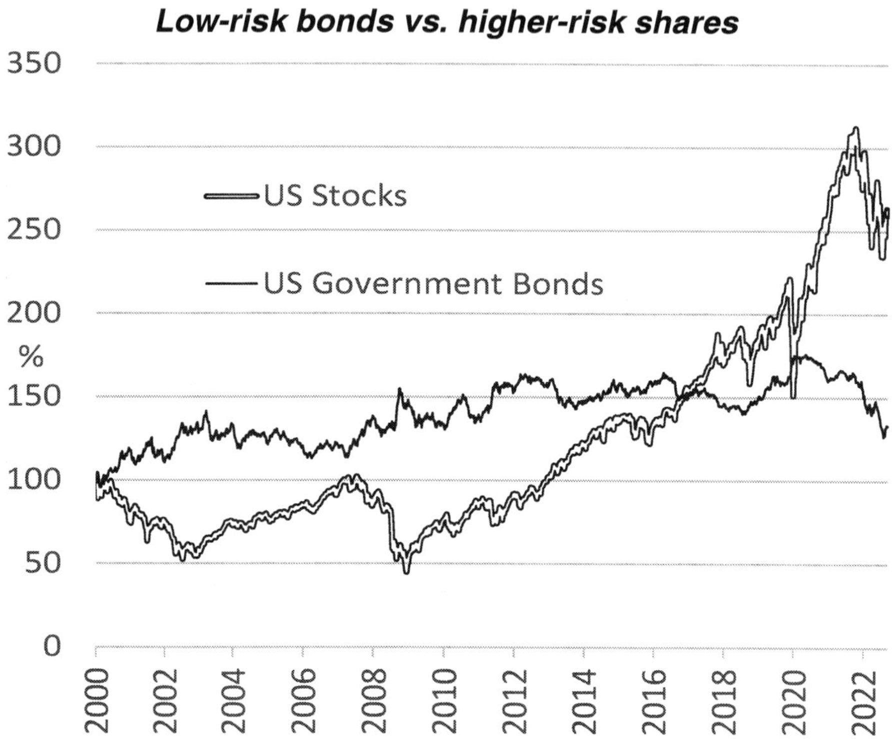

Technical info about this chart in case you want it:
US Stocks data: the weekly last-price of the S&P 500 benchmark (.SP500).
US Government Bonds data: US 10-year Treasury bid yield (last) weekly benchmark (US 10YT=RR), Inverted for the chart. Data source: Refinitiv, November 2022.

Shares are generally higher risk. Not only do they move up and down more violently, but the range within which they rose and fell over 20 years is much greater: they fell by more than 50% in 2009, but rose above the 300% mark in 2021.

During positive economic times, shares have tended to rise while bonds have not performed as positively.

During negative economic times, such as in 2008 and 2020, shares have fallen sharply while bonds rose.

Bonds tend to perform fairly steadily but don't tend to rise much over time.

Shares have many more up and down movements (volatility), but have tended to rise over longer periods of time.

The performance of both shares and bonds would look very different if you changed the starting point. This chart ONLY shows how they performed relative to their respective values in 2000.

What are shares and bonds?

I cover this in more detail in chapter 17. For now, shares (also referred to as "stocks" or "equity") and bonds are two different ways in which a company can raise money for, say, building a new factory.

With shares, the company directors sell a portion of the company to investors. With bonds, the company is borrowing money from investors, which it will pay back after a set period of time.

If you own shares in Microsoft, then you are a part-owner of that company. The price you paid for those shares goes up and down making your investment rise and fall. As a shareholder, you're also entitled to a share in the profits if the company chooses to pay a dividend to shareholders.

Shares issued by big, profitable companies in stable economies (such as Microsoft or HSBC) are less risky than companies with high debt burdens, low profits, or those which are based in a country with an unstable economic environment such as Russia or, in recent years, Brazil.

Bonds are loans investors make to governments or companies. A bond might be issued (sold to investors) with a face value of

£100. That means that after a period of time, the bond issuer (the government or company that sold the bond) will pay the investor £100.

Generally speaking, the investor pays less than £100 to buy the bond. This means they'll get a bit of profit to look forward to, and may receive an interest payment each year until the bond matures i.e., when the bond's life finishes and they get the £100 back.

Most bonds pay a fixed rate of interest, which is referred to as the "coupon". I explain what bonds and other asset classes are, and how they might be useful, in chapter 17.

Bonds issued by big, profitable companies or governments in stable economies, such as Microsoft or the US government, are seen as relatively low risk and, therefore, don't pay much interest. Riskier companies or governments have to offer higher rates of interest to persuade investors to buy the bonds.

Bottom line

If risk is respected and not feared, it can work in your favour.

15 How much risk should you take?

Here are some questions to ask yourself to help gauge what level of risk might be appropriate for you:

- How comfortable are you with risk?
- How close are you to retirement (assuming that's what you're investing for)?
- How much do you have invested already?

How comfortable are you with risk?

The intention of this book is to help you in your journey to find an investment solution that works for you in such a way that your money largely takes care of itself leaving you to get on with your life without worrying about your investments.

If you don't feel comfortable with risk, then minimise the amount of risk in your portfolio (remembering that it's impossible to eliminate it completely). It's that simple.

It will mean that the potential for growth in your investments is lower, but that's worth it for your peace of mind. If you start getting stressed about your investments, then it defeats the object of this book and you're more likely to start making poor decisions.

On the other hand, if you fully appreciate that higher-risk investments are more likely to fall and rise a lot over the short-term (a year or two)...
AND you have enough time for that not to matter...
AND those more volatile price movements wouldn't cause you anxiety, then it could make more sense for you to invest in a medium- or higher-risk set of investments, which tend to offer greater potential gains over time.

How close are you to retirement?

I'm using retirement as the investment goal here as doing so keeps things relatively simple for the purposes of this book.

Your specific investment goal could be the deposit on a house, paying for school or university fees or a plethora of other targets.

These are all issues that an IFA with whole-of-market coverage, can help you to focus on and plan for.

The younger you are, the more time your investments have to capture the general long-term trend of rising share prices. What this means is that the risk of short-term sharp falls in share prices is less relevant to you.

Shares have tended to follow an eight-to-12-year cycle of gradual rises over many years followed by sharp falls over a year or two before the process is repeated.

The longer you can leave the investments, the better. By which token, the reverse is also true. As you get closer to retirement (or the point at which you need to cash in some of your investments), the less you can afford to have your investments at risk of a sharp fall in value.

Here are some rough guidelines to your age and how much risk might be appropriate for you.

Young person just starting a career

An enviable position to be in. You might be broke but you have the most precious and valuable commodity on your side, time.

As such, it's an ideal opportunity to start investing something every month, not matter how small the amount. It will pay handsomely in years to come.

If you can afford to buy a beer or two at the weekend, you can afford to put £20 away each month (preferably more, but put SOMETHING into your investments each month).

This is also the position in which the greatest amount of calculated and considered investment risk probably can be taken. And by that, I mean more shares (which tend to have more price ups and downs) and fewer bonds (which have fewer ups and downs) i.e., "higher-risk" portfolio. I'll explain what that looks like in chapter 17.

More than 10 years from retirement

Assuming that your circumstances don't change, the risk level you're comfortable with at 25 is unlikely to change much while you're more than 10 years away from retirement (assuming, once again, that retirement is your investment goal).

10 years or less from retirement

If you're going to need your investments to provide a post-retirement income, then this is the point at which you should be considering reducing the level of risk in your investment portfolio.

This would mean transitioning your investments from higher risk and capital growth (i.e., rising in value) investments to lower-risk and income-generating investments.

Reducing risk as you age

The following is a simple example of how to manage how much risk there is in your investment portfolio as you approach retirement.

Assumptions include:

- You are investing for your retirement
- You will retire between the ages of 65 and 67
- You will be relying on your investments to pay for your retirement lifestyle.

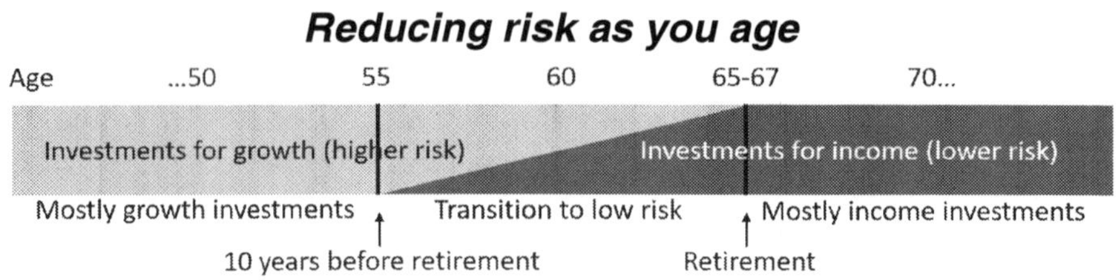

The point, as usual, is a simple one. The more time you have before you need to dip into your investments, the more risk you can afford to take with it.

As you get to within 10 years of the date at which you'll be living off your investments (e.g. retirement), it usually makes sense to start reducing the higher-risk investments, such as shares, and increasing the lower-risk ones, such as bonds.

Retired and needing an income stream to live off

The opportunity for higher risk and capital growth investments has largely gone. Depending on how much you have invested and what other income sources you have, the focus is likely to be more on low-risk, income-generating investments.

However, that doesn't mean that you shouldn't have any shares. If I were building an income-generating portfolio, I'd consider a mix of relatively low-risk shares that generate decent yields (i.e., income-generating), as well as low-risk corporate bonds that generate decent dividends (income again).

Portfolios set according to levels of risk

There are three broad levels of risk across investment portfolios:

- Lower risk
- Medium risk
- Higher risk

And there's one that's designed to generate a revenue stream but less likely to grow over time:

- Income-generating

Many banks and investment firms have a larger range of risk-rated portfolios with alluring names like "Defensive" (i.e., lower-risk) or "Dynamic" (i.e., higher-risk). These could provide even lower than my "Lower risk" portfolios or higher risk than my "higher risk" portfolios, or somewhere between. They also have nonsense names like "Adventurous", "Cautious" or "Frontier".

Many of those banks and investment firms will talk about providing an investment portfolio that's "designed to meet your needs", "best matches your needs" or even "tailored to your needs".

From my experience, the reality is that they have a handful of risk-rated portfolios which, between them, can be sufficient to roughly meet the risk appetites of most investors... except that the fees are too high and the performance tends to be awful.

I'll share with you the steps I take to avoid being ripped off.

These are the stages I'll cover:

- Draw on all the research of the big banks and investment firms
- Find funds that will allow me to create low-cost, passive versions of those portfolios
- Determine which level of risk-return is most appropriate for me
- Choose the appropriate portfolio in terms of risk and the amount of money to invest
- Go through a step-by-step process of setting up the portfolios.

Bottom line

Complete the risk assessment questionnaire in the next chapter to help determine what level of risk might be right for you.

16 Risk assessment questionnaire

Many fund managers and banks have a variety of short questionnaires on their respective websites which are designed to give you an indication of the level of risk that's right for you.

In my opinion, the trouble with most of these questionnaires is that they tend to be too short and to lead the person taking the assessment to be overly cautious.

As I mentioned earlier in this book, risk is not a bad thing in itself. Too much risk for you is bad, but so is too little.

I wanted to avoid these pitfalls in my questionnaire. I therefore created it by basing it on a shortened version of the excellent questionnaire created by John Grable and Ruth Lytton as visiting professors at the University of Missouri.

The questionnaire was published in the Financial Services Review. You can find the full version here: https://pfp.missouri.edu/research/investment-risk-tolerance-assessment/

My version of the questionnaire is different from the original because I've made the following assumptions:

- You are investing for your retirement or a similarly significant nest egg or event
- You are at least 10 years away from needing to use the money you've invested
- You have followed the steps outlined in Part 3 - Laying the foundations.

Also, I've created my own scoring for this questionnaire which allows for the fact that I have three levels of risk in my low-cost investment portfolios: lower, medium and higher.

Remember, this isn't a school test

This is an indication of what might be right for you. The more honest you are in your answers, the more likely it will be for the outcome to provide a reasonable indication of what level of risk might be right for you.

The questionnaire

Make a note of your answer for each of the following and work out your score at the end.

1. In general, how would your best friend describe you as a risk-taker?

a. A real gambler
b. Willing to take risks after completing adequate research
c. Cautious
d. A real risk-avoider

2. You are on a TV game show and can choose one of the following. Which would you take?

a. £1,000 in cash
b. A 50% chance of winning £5,000
c. A 25% chance of winning £10,000
d. A 5% chance of winning £100,000

3. You have just finished saving for a once-in-a-lifetime holiday. Three weeks before you plan to leave, you lose your job. You would:

a. Cancel the holiday
b. Take a much more modest holiday
c. Go as scheduled, reasoning that you need the time to prepare for a job search
d. Extend your holiday, because this might be your last chance to go first-class

4. If you unexpectedly received £20,000 to invest, what would you do?

a. Deposit it in a bank account, keep as cash, or buy premium bonds

b. Invest it in low-risk, high-quality bonds or bond mutual funds

c. Invest it in company shares or investment funds

5. In terms of experience, how comfortable are you investing in company shares or funds that consist of company shares?

a. Not at all comfortable

b. Somewhat comfortable

c. Very comfortable

6. When you think of the word "risk", which of the following words comes to mind first?

a. Loss

b. Uncertainty

c. Opportunity

d. Thrill

7. Imagine this scenario: Some experts are predicting prices of assets such as gold, jewels, collectibles, and real estate (hard assets) to increase in value; bond prices may fall, however, experts tend to agree that government bonds are relatively safe. Most of your investment assets are now in high-interest government bonds. What would you do?

a. Hold the bonds

b. Sell the bonds, put half the proceeds into a savings account, and the other half into hard assets

c. Sell the bonds and put the total proceeds into hard assets

d. Sell the bonds, put all the money into hard assets, and borrow additional money to buy more

8. Given the best- and worst-case returns of the four investment choices below, which would you prefer?

a. £200 gain best case; £0 gain/loss worst case

b. £800 gain best case; £200 loss worst case

c. £2,600 gain best case; £800 loss worst case
d. £4,800 gain best case; £2,400 loss worst case

9. In addition to whatever you own, you have been given £1,000. You are now asked to choose between:
a. A sure gain of £500
b. A 50% chance to gain £1,000 and a 50% chance to gain nothing

10. In addition to whatever you own, you have been given £2,000. You are now asked to choose between:
a. A sure loss of £500
b. A 50% chance to lose £1,000 and a 50% chance to lose nothing

11. Suppose a relative left you an inheritance of £100,000, stipulating in the will that you invest ALL the money in ONE of the following choices. Which one would you select?
a. A savings account or premium bonds
b. An investment fund that owns shares and bonds
c. A portfolio of shares of 15 companies
d. Commodities like gold, silver, and oil

12. If you had to invest £20,000, which of the following investment choices would you find most appealing?
a. 60% in low-risk investments, 30% in medium-risk investments, 10% in high risk investments
b. 30% in low-risk investments, 40% in medium-risk investments, 30% in high-risk investments
c. 10% in low-risk investments, 40% in medium-risk investments, 50% in high-risk investments

13. Your trusted friend and neighbour, an experienced geologist, is putting together a group of investors to fund an exploratory gold mining venture. The venture could pay back 50- to 100-times the investment if successful. If the mine is a bust, the entire investment is worthless. Your friend estimates the chance of success is only 20%. If you had the money, how much would you invest?

a. Nothing
b. One month's salary
c. Three month's salary
d. Six month's salary

14. On a scale from one to five (where one is lowest and five highest), how would you rate your overall understanding of personal finance and money-management concepts and practices?

a. 1
b. 2
c. 3
d. 4
e. 5

15. Suppose you had £100 in a savings account and the interest rate was 2% per year. After five years, how much do you think you would have in the account if you left the money to grow?

a. More than £102
b. Exactly £102
c. Less than £102
d. Do not know

16. Imagine that the interest rate on your savings account was 1% per year and inflation was 2% per year. After one year, how much would you be able to buy with the money in this account?

a. More than today
b. Exactly the same
c. Less than today
d. Do not know

17. Please say whether this is true or false: "Buying a single company's stock usually provides a safer return than a stock mutual fund".

a. TRUE
b. FALSE
c. Do not know

Calculating your score

Now work out your total score using the following table. For example, if you answered "b" to question 1, you would earn two points.

	a	b	c	d	e
1	3	2	1	0	
2	0	1	2	3	
3	0	1	2	3	
4	0	1	2		
5	0	1	2		
6	0	1	2	3	
7	0	1	2	3	
8	0	1	2	3	
9	0	2			
10	0	2			
11	0	1	2	3	
12	0	1	2		
13	0	1	2	3	
14	0	1	2	3	4
15	3	1	0	0	
16	0	1	3	0	
17	0	3	1		

Which of the following indicative brackets does your score fall into?

- 32-47 Higher risk
- 20-31 Medium risk
- 0-19 Lower risk

Bottom line

This score isn't a hard-and-fast outcome, it's an indication of what sort of risk level might be right for you. The point being, don't take too little or too much risk.

PART FIVE

Asset Classes Explained

17 Different types of investments

In this section, I'll explain what the different types of investments or asset classes are, what they do and why people have them.

I've left this explanation until after explaining how you're being ripped off in the hope that you'll be suitably incentivised to read this!

It might sound boring, but it's worth a read. It will help you better understand why you might have particular investments within your portfolio.

Why it's helpful to know this

In my portfolios, I don't need to choose individual assets. This is taken care of by buying the low-cost funds that I prefer.

However, by having a basic understanding of asset classes (e.g., cash, gold, shares, bonds), you're less likely to worry unduly when things don't go up as fast as you thought they would or go down more than you thought they would.

Both these scenarios will happen sooner or later, that's just the nature of investing, so being mentally prepared can save a good deal of stress.

What assets go into the different portfolios?

The following chart gives an indication of the risk levels associated with different asset classes, and which assets tend to be favoured by the portfolios that I set up later in the book.

This chart just gives you an idea of the sort of investments that are most likely to be in each portfolio and the approximate level of risk.

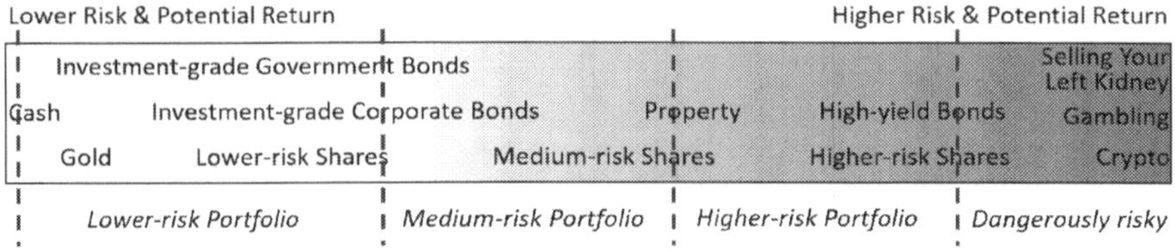

Asset classes within the portfolios

The following is a brief outline of each asset class and why you might want to hold them. It will help you in your quest to set up an investment portfolio that largely looks after itself.

Cash

Cash can include both savings with instant access and ready cash in your pocket.

The cash that I'm more concerned with here is the cash that you hold in your investment account (I'll explain what an investment account is later) rather than using it to buy funds, shares or bonds. Here's why you might keep some cash in that investment account.

Paying fees

Holding investments incurs fees. It might be the Ongoing Charges Figure (OCF) that the funds charge, the annual fee that the "platform" (i.e., the company with which you hold the investments charges) or a range of other fees. But fees there shall be.

I always want some cash in a portfolio so that the ongoing fees and transaction costs can be met without my having to sell assets in a hurry to cover those costs.

Selling a car or a house in a hurry means that the buyer can offer a lower price than might otherwise be seen as fair value. The same applies to investments.

Waiting for the next financial year to top up ISAs and pensions

If tax-efficient investment "wrappers" like ISAs and pensions are available to me, I'll use them.

It might be that I've used my annual allowance in one or both and want to wait a few months before putting money into investments so that I can keep everything as tax-efficient as possible (i.e., legally minimising the amount of tax I have to pay).

Offsetting falls or rises in other assets - "hedging"

Holding cash can "hedge your bets" i.e., if your shares or bonds go down, then the cash you hold will stay at much the same value over the short term. This has the effect of reducing the loss across your entire portfolio.

The same works in reverse. The more cash you hold, the less you'll benefit from rises in the shares or bonds that you hold.

Reasons for holding cash

- To pay ongoing fees/ charges - every portfolio should have at least a small amount of cash
- You are waiting for a tax-efficient moment to buy investments in your pension or ISA
- You expect asset prices to go down in value, perhaps because inflation and bills are rising faster than wages. The more likely you think asset price falls are, the more cash you might be inclined to hold.

Government bonds - lower-risk rated ones

Lower-risk bonds are referred to as "investment grade." This applies to bonds issued (sold) by governments or companies that are considered to be financially robust.

Higher-risk bonds are referred to as "sub-investment grade", "high-yield" or "junk" bonds. They are riskier and offer a higher yield to persuade investors to buy them. Some of them are so risky that they're junk and you'll be lucky to get any of your money back.

Higher-risk bonds can be issued by companies or governments that have less financial stability or that are in countries with lower stability.

For example, a company with small profits and loads of debt would be considered higher-risk in any country. Meanwhile, bonds issued by governments of countries with unstable political or economic environments would also be considered higher-risk.

If you buy a government bond, you are effectively lending money to that government. Many governments don't raise enough money through taxation to meet all their commitments in social welfare, roads, police, etc. So, they sell loads of bonds.

There are other reasons why they sell bonds, such as maintaining stable financial markets. You can read more about these at Investopedia.com.

A bond usually has a fixed period of time before the bond issuer (the government in this case) pays the face value of the bond back to the investor (see the Glossary for more info if you want).

This period of time can be three, five, 10 or 30 years. The longer the period, the more risk the investor is taking by having their money tied up in the bond. With that higher risk comes a higher return, either through a higher interest payment or a cheaper price for buying the bond.

Most government bonds pay a fixed annual interest payment, called a coupon. Some will pay a coupon that rises and falls roughly in line with inflation. These bonds are referred to as index-linked bonds, which is why they are often used to...

Counteract inflation

If you think the rate of inflation is likely to rise, you might be more likely to buy index-linked bonds because the return on those bonds would rise more or less in line with inflation. If you think inflation is likely to fall, you might go for fixed-rate bonds because they would continue to pay the same coupon even though interest rates might follow inflation rates downwards.

Income-generation

A bond that pays a fixed or index-linked coupon can be appropriate for you if you want your investments to generate an income.

Risk reduction

Bonds issued by stable governments such as those of the USA, EU and the UK (yes, I do include the UK government despite its seemingly endless shenanigans) tend to be seen as relative low risk (the UK's risk level has increased in recent years thanks to some spectacular political incompetence).

These bond issuers have a strong track record of meeting their coupon and repayment obligations. As a result, their prices tend not to move up and down as much as the prices of bonds or shares issued by companies.

This can make holding government bonds appropriate for you if you prefer a very low-risk approach to investing. It can also help to reduce the effect that a downturn in the economy could have on your overall portfolio; share prices could fall more sharply in such circumstances.

Reasons for holding low-risk government bonds

- To adjust for how you think inflation is likely to pan out
- To generate an income
- To reduce the level of risk in your portfolio to meet your preference

Government bonds - higher-risk rated ones

Argentina and Russia have failed to meet their repayment obligations in recent years. This is referred to as defaulting. As a result, the risk associated with their government bonds is much higher, meaning that they have to pay higher coupons to persuade investors to accept the risk that comes with owning their bonds.

Other factors such as a relatively unstable political or economic environment, or a currency that can go up and down a lot also increase the level of risk that comes with the relevant country's government bonds.

Around the low-risk end of the scale are US government bonds, referred to as Treasuries. Towards the upper end are Russian bonds. Spread across between them are all the other countries whose governments issue bonds.

The thing to remember (should you want to) is which countries are recognised as offering lower-risk bonds. The rest can be considered higher risk. The funds I use take care of that distinction for me.

If you know what you're doing as a sophisticated investor with an understanding of risk pricing, government credentials and economic outlook, then higher-risk government bonds might be for you. But then, if that's you, you're probably not reading this book.

Reasons for holding high-risk government bonds

- To add a higher-risk and higher potential-return asset to your portfolio.

Corporate bonds - lower-risk rated ones

Lots of companies raise money by issuing bonds. Some of those companies are household names with big profits and a solid outlook. As a result, their bonds are adjudged to carry lower risk, by rating agencies (the folk who investigate and rate how high or low the level of risk is with companies and governments).

Reasons for holding lower-risk corporate bonds
The same as holding lower-risk government bonds.
The difference is that corporate bonds tend to be slightly higher risk and offer slightly higher returns.

Corporate bonds - higher risk
These don't feature much in the portfolios I've put together for this book because they're too risky.

Reasons for holding higher-risk corporate bonds
- Higher potential return

Company shares (or "stocks" or "equity")
If you buy shares in a company, you own a part of that company and are entitled to a share of any profits that are paid to investors in the form of annual payments known as "dividends".

Companies come in all shapes and sizes with almost every level of risk you can think of. Massive, profit-generating conglomerates in growing markets tend to carry lower levels of risk, which makes them attractive to lots of investors and, therefore, more expensive to buy.

By contrast, companies with great ideas and lots of debt but little revenue carry a big risk of going bust. Some make it big, sending their respective share prices rocketing.

This is where passive funds can be ideal.

With the right passive fund, you pay low fees but get access to a range of companies. In investment speak, a passive fund can provide a diversified (i.e., mixed) portfolio. But you can still select one or more passive funds to meet your needs.

I include shares in all of the portfolios I talk about later in this book. All my portfolios are invested entirely in low-cost, diversified, passive funds.

Reasons for holding shares

- Lower-risk rated companies: can provide a low- to medium-risk, predictable income stream or lower potential return on investment.
- Medium-risk rated companies: can provide access to more potential for growth in your investments over a number of years. Prices will go down and up during that time.
- Higher-risk rated companies: these tend to be for investors with money invested elsewhere, or who are sufficiently cash-rich and debt-free to be able to invest in some risky companies that might come good but could also slump in value.

Gold

This isn't as attractive as you might think, which is why the portfolios I copy don't include it.

It pays no interest or dividend, there's always more of it being dug out of the ground and added to the total global stock of the stuff, it has to be verified as genuine, and it has to be kept safe from theft.

Buying actual gold might make you feel good, but you've almost certainly lost money on the transaction unless the price of gold shoots up.

Why? Because the person most likely to buy that gold from you is the person who sold it to you. They will have added a profit margin when they sold it to you (you overpaid), and they won't pay you what they can sell it for (they'll underpay to buy it back from you).

Buying a passive fund that tracks the price of gold does make sense for some investors. You don't need to worry about where to keep the stuff or whether it's genuine. It's also going to be relatively easy to sell your holdings in the passive fund.

I've included gold funds in the list of funds that I like because you might decide to have gold in your portfolio.

"Store of value"

There are two main benefits to gold. Firstly, its price has tended to move similarly to the rate of inflation. In simple terms, this is because when people see prices rising quickly, they are less likely to want to hold cash which will lose its value.

A better alternative can be something that holds its value, such as gold. Hence, it's referred to as a store of value.

This also works in reverse: when inflation falls, there can be less demand for gold sending its price down.

This doesn't always work.

The value of gold goes up and down due to a variety of factors. These can include the value of the dollar (gold is priced in dollars), how much gold is being dug up by gold miners, and any number of things that might be going on in the world.

Diversification

That's why the second reason for holding gold is important: it's a diversifier. Gold's price doesn't tend to go up and down at the same time that shares and bonds do.

Holding a small amount of gold can help to reduce the effect that price falls and rises have on your overall portfolio. It's not for everyone, but it can have its place.

Reasons for holding gold

- Store of value to counter the effects of inflation.
- Diversifier to counter the price falls and rises of shares and bonds (as happened during the Covid pandemic).

Property funds

This isn't owning actual property (which is referred to as "direct ownership"). In this case, I'm referring to owning, surprise surprise, shares in a passive fund that owns a range of actual properties.

Being a landlord sucks. If you want to do that, be prepared for hassle and expense. I know several landlords and they'd all happily get rid of their properties if they could find a way of generating a similar income but with less hassle.

If you're good at it and enjoy it, go for it. For me, there's too much risk (bad tenants, leaking pipes, expensive mortgages, rising interest rates, etc.)

By contrast, property funds can offer diversification in your overall portfolio without the negatives of being a landlord. The ups and downs of shares and bonds have limited relevance to the prices of property.

So, if your overall portfolio is hit by a broad fall in the prices of shares or bonds, your investment in a property fund is likely to behave differently, reducing the effect of price changes on your overall investment portfolio.

There is one massive potential negative of investing in a property fund, the occasional difficulty of selling your holding in that fund.

Property is illiquid i.e., it takes time and money to sell. If property prices slump, the property fund can't sell its holdings in the properties that it owns without taking huge losses compared to what it paid for them.

However, when that does happen, lots of investors want to sell their holdings in the investment fund because the fund's value will fall in line with the drop in property prices.

This creates a dilemma for the property fund managers. Over recent years, a number of property funds have faced this exact situation and have addressed it by banning investors from selling their holdings in the property fund i.e., a suspension in trading.

As an investor, there's nothing you can do about this. You just have to wait until property prices recover and the fund lifts its suspension. This can take months or even years.

The lesson from this is twofold.

First, including a property fund is only appropriate if you can afford to hold it for the long-term e.g., 10 years.

Second, I wouldn't allow property to dominate my portfolio; a small allocation can be appropriate either to generate income or to diversify my overall portfolio.

Reasons to hold property

- Diversification.

Cryptocurrencies - throwing your money away

Cryptocurrencies such as Bitcoin and Ethereum are about as sensible as selling your organs. Don't throw your money away.

Why are crypto currencies so horrendous? Because:

- There's no underlying revenue stream (i.e., profit or sales)
- There's no way of knowing if the value is likely to go up or down
- The trading platforms are notoriously unreliable and subject to corruption and theft
- Criminals use it for money laundering
- Governments have massive incentives to ban them (some already have).

Reasons for buying cryptocurrencies

- A fraudster or someone who doesn't know what they're talking about has persuaded you it's a good idea. It's not. It's a terrible idea. Don't do it.

Foreign currency

I include this because you might think that it makes sense to have currencies. You might think it's quite exciting. Well, it's certainly exciting because it's one of the quickest ways to lose a lot of money.

I don't include currency purchases, even US dollars, in my portfolios. There's no point as far as I'm concerned.

If you want to trade currencies then read at least three books on the subject. Start with Robbie Burns' book, *The Naked Trader's Guide to Spread Betting*.

Reasons for buying foreign currency

- None for the purposes of this book.

Others

There are loads of other asset classes I haven't covered because they're irrelevant to what I'm trying to achieve: a low-cost investment portfolio that largely takes care of itself and gives little cause for me to worry.

If you want to play around with derivatives, overlays, leverage, etc. then feel free, but make sure you know what you're doing.

With that in mind, here's a sobering thought on these investment classes. A former colleague of mine used to run a team of traders for a massive bank. Traders are ruthless, not caring who loses out so long as they make money. My former colleague's team members all operated on this maxim: "If you don't know who in the trade is being screwed, it's you".

However, if there's an investment class that you think I should have covered then visit InvestWithoutBeingRippedOff.com and see if I've written about it there. If I haven't, contact me via the website and I'll have a look at it.

Bottom line

I prefer a diversified portfolio and I will NEVER be fooled into buying any cryptocurrency. I've worked too hard for my money.

PART SIX

Tax-Efficient Investing

18 Tax wrappers

I'm all for paying taxes that are due. Everyone should pay their taxes, even the big companies that manipulate their head office, revenue recognition and anything else to avoid paying taxes that the ordinary Joe on the street simply has to pay.

However, when a government sets up a situation to encourage investment and planning for your future by giving tax-related incentives, then it would be daft not to take advantage.

In the US, tax allowances on personal profits made from selling investments are quite generous. You have to have made a fairly decent chunk of money before you have to start paying tax on it.

It's complex, so get professional advice to make sure you're doing what you should in a tax-efficient manner.

In the UK, my understanding is that the allowances are less generous but there are ways of investing that are tax-efficient. Some people refer to these as tax-free, which they are not. At some point the taxman (or woman) has intervened or will intervene, but in a much-reduced way.

Important

All that follows is my understanding at the time of writing in 2023. **It must not be taken as advice.** Also, please check for changes in legislation and get professional advice if you need it before taking any investment or tax-related decisions.

The UK's tax "wrappers"

There are two main vehicles/wrappers that a "keep-it-simple" investor like me is interested in:

- **Individual Savings Accounts** (**ISAs**)
- Pensions. For the purposes of this book, I mostly refer to **Self-Invested Personal Pensions** (**SIPPs**) because I understand them and they afford me the opportunity to control every aspect of what I'm investing in.

However, the principles might be applicable to other types of pension, such as Personal Pensions, Retirement Accounts, Group Personal Pensions, Small Self-Administered Pension Schemes and whatnot.

The other acronym is **GIA which stands for General Investment Account.** You have an annual tax-free allowance on the profit made across these accounts. This allowance was slashed by 50%

in 2023 to £6,000 per person per financial year. Every penny that investments make above that in a non-tax-efficient investment will be taxed.

By contrast, any profits or growth made in an ISA is not taxed, while those made in a SIPP are only subject to tax once you start taking money out of the SIPP (unless you hit a massive threshold of around £1million at the time of writing).

The UK Government wants you to make money in SIPPs and ISAs because it means you'll be less likely to need social welfare from the government in later life.

And, remember, the ***full*** state pension is only £10,400 a year.

ISA

Maximum annual contribution

At the time of writing in the financial year-ending April 2024, you can put up to £20,000 each tax year into ISA investments. You can have as many ISAs as you like, but the total added to all of them combined cannot exceed £20,000 in one financial year.

There are two types of ISA that I'll focus on:

- "Cash ISAs" for cash earning a low rate of interest
- "Stocks and Shares" or "S&S ISAs" for investments in shares, bonds, funds, etc.

The main difference between an ISA and a SIPP is the point at which the taxman is or is not interested. This is because the money that goes into an ISA has already been taxed, e.g. your salary after tax deductions.

Let's look at each of them in more detail.

Cash ISA
I don't like cash ISAs. They pay low interest and often come with notice periods and withdrawal fees.

If I want to put money into an interest-paying savings account then I'll do so as part of my cash buffer, not as part of my investment portfolio.

Stocks and shares ISA
The first thing to note is that a stocks and shares ISA is not limited to "stocks and shares" which, in any case, are the same thing.

This type of ISA allows you to invest in shares, bonds and funds – both passive and active. And that covers everything we need for the purposes of this book.

How do you use an ISA?
Think of the ISA as a shopping basket. Once you set up an ISA, you can browse the funds on offer and buy the ones that suit your needs e.g., £1,000 in a global index tracker, £1,000 in a corporate bond fund, etc.

I provide step-by-step examples with screenshots in Part 8 - Setting up investments.

The point is that any growth, dividends or other profits made in your ISA cannot be taxed.

The supermarket equivalent would be a shopping basket in which everything you bought was free from sales tax or value-added tax (VAT). It's not quite the same, but it gives you the idea.

Transferring money from one ISA to another
You can transfer money from one ISA to another if you want to. None of these transfers will count towards the £20,000 annual top-up allowance.

For most ISAs, you can also withdraw money which you can put back in later in the same financial year.

For example, if you withdraw £1,000 from an ISA account, you can place £20,000 into ISA accounts that year PLUS the £1,000 that you withdrew in that same financial year.

No carrying over unused allowance from previous years

You can't carry any of one year's allowance over into the next tax year though. If you don't contribute the full £20,000 in one financial year, it makes no difference to the following year's allowance.

No tax on withdrawals

When you take money out of the ISA, there's no tax to pay on any profits.

A few people who have dedicated a good deal of time and effort into researching investments have managed to turn their ISA investments into more than a million pounds. These ISA millionaires constitute a tiny minority, but it shows how valuable the ISA tax-free basket can be.

No restrictions on withdrawals

As far as the law and taxman are concerned, you can withdraw whatever you like, whenever you like, from an ISA.

SIPP

A Self-Invested Pension Plan (SIPP), is another investment shopping basket. It has a higher limit than an ISA on the amount of money you can put in each year.

For the tax year-ending March 2024, you could put up to a total of £60,000 a year into your SIPP (or SIPPs if you have several). But this amount cannot be more than your annual earnings which cannot include some revenues you might have, such as rental income.

You can use some allowance from previous years

If you haven't used the allowance from the previous three years (i.e., you haven't contributed the maximum over the past three years), you might be able to add it to your allowance for the current year.

However, any amount you add to your SIPP in a given year cannot exceed your total taxable earnings for that one year. Also, there might be a minimum amount of contribution you have to have made over the preceding four years or so.

I tried to come up with an example but it's too complex to cover without saying something that might not apply to you. Instead, here is a link to the UK Government website that addresses this sort of thing: www.gov.uk/personal-pension-your-rights

Maximum annual contribution

As I mentioned, you cannot put an amount greater than your annual gross income (before tax) into your SIPP.

Someone earning £30,000 (in income that qualifies) a year cannot put more than £30,000 a year into their SIPP (or in total across their SIPPs if they have several). This applies even if you've inherited £50,000.

Withdrawals are subject to tax (with a generous allowance)

Now for the sting in the tail. When you withdraw money from a SIPP, the taxman wants to know everything. He also restricts the ways in which you can withdraw money.

Before you get to this stage you should seek advice from a whole-of-market IFA because the choices will depend on your unique circumstances.

One of the factors to consider is how best to use the 25% tax-free allowance when taking money out of a SIPP (or "drawing down" as financial folk prefer to call it).

Do you take that entire 25% upfront and then set up the rest as part-annuity, part-income, both of which would be subject to tax? Or do you do any number of other combinations?

The not-terribly-helpful answer, once again, is that it depends on your unique circumstances. Professional advice could well be in order here.

No access before you reach at least 55

SIPPs are called Self-Invested Pension Plans for a reason. They're for your later life. Hence the government doesn't want you squandering money you have in them before you are at least 55 until 2028 and at least 57 thereafter.

You can continue to contribute and get tax-back benefits after that age, but those benefits stop as soon as you withdraw any money.

Rip-Off Tip-Off

For many UK taxpayers, the age at which you can access your pension will be 57 under current projections. That age could climb.

ISA vs. SIPP

The following table provides a quick summary of the pros and cons of ISAs and SIPPs. It more or less boils down to much easier access to money in an ISA against top-up incentives added to a SIPP.

They both have their purposes, which is why I have both.

Summary ISA vs. SIPP comparison

	ISA	SIPP
Maximum annual contribution	£20,000	It depends (sorry!) Your total gross salary OR £60,000 (plus carry over), whichever is lower.
Contribution carry-over	None	Unused contribution from previous three tax years.
Tax rebate on money you contribute	0%	Your marginal rate (e.g., 20%, 40%, 45%).
"Turbocharge" (see next chapter)	Not possible	Possible
What you can invest in	Shares, bonds and funds	Shares, bonds and funds
When you can withdraw	Whenever you like	After you reach a specific age
How you can withdraw	Cash (i.e., flexible)	Restricted (i.e., less flexible)
Tax-free withdrawals	100% tax-free	25% tax-free

Bottom line

Don't unnecessarily hand a chunk of your annual growth to the taxman every year. Make use of ISAs and SIPPs.

19 Turbo-charge your pension

This is what I did because it made sense for me in my circumstances.

It's like snowballing

What it boils down to is adding money to your SIPP, getting an automatic top-up from the government, then claiming any further top-ups at the end of the year and putting those into the SIPP which, in turn, generate further top-ups from the government. Then repeat the process each year.

The government is essentially giving tax back to you that you've paid. They do this because the more you have in your private pension, the less of a financial burden you're likely to be to the state when you retire.

As the chart below shows, turbocharging your pension could help it to grow by 20% or even 40% or more over 10 years, just by making use of the UK government's pension investment incentive.

As always, it can be wise to get some professional advice on what's right for you because, as mentioned, there are restrictions on how and when you can take money out of (draw down from) your SIPP.

The sort of difference turbocharging could make

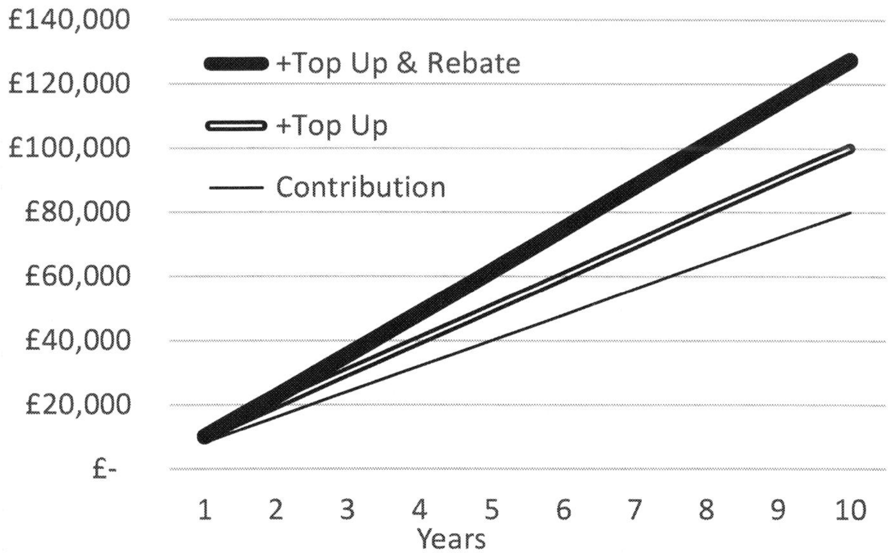

In this example, I'm adding £8,000 a year to my investments.

Thin line = no top-ups or rebates are claimed.
Final total = £80,000.

Double line = the money goes into a SIPP and automatically earns a 20% top-up from the UK government.
Final total = £100,000 (see example 1 below).

Thick line = As well as the 20% top-up, I might also be able to claim a further 20% rebate for being a higher-rate tax payer. I add that rebate to my pension contributions the following year.
Final total = £137,934 (see example 2, below).

Here are two hypothetical examples of how it might work for:

1. **Someone who has paid a lower rate of tax, 20%,** on the money they're putting into their pension. This person will get a 20% top-up of the money they put into their pension automatically added by the government.

2. **Someone who has paid a higher rate of tax, 40%,** on the money they're putting into their pension. As well as the automatic 20% top-up, this person can claim a further 20% rebate in their HMRC self-assessment at the end of that financial year.

Rip-Off Tip-Off

It's up to me to make sure that I only claim a top-up or tax rebate on money that I have paid tax on and which adds up to no more than my qualifying earnings for the financial year in question. You can find out more about the tax relief on pensions contributions here: https://www.gov.uk/tax-on-your-private-pension/pension-tax-relief

Example 1, Basic-rate tax rate payers

Year One

Make annual contribution to my SIPP of, say, £8,000.
Watch the £2,000 top up get added to my SIPP by the government a couple of months later.

Total added to my SIPP in that year
£10,000: £8,000 of my money + £2,000 government top up.

Year Two

Make annual £8,000 contribution to my SIPP.

Watch the £2,000 top up get added to my SIPP by the government.

Total added to my SIPP in that year
£10,000 giving a running total after two years of £20,000

Year Three

Make annual £8,000 contribution to my SIPP.
Watch the £2,000 top up get added to my SIPP by the government.

Total added to my SIPP in that year
£10,000, giving a running total after three years of £30,000
And so on.

Example 2: Higher-tax rate payers

Year One

Make annual contribution to my SIPP of, say, £8,000.
Watch the £2,000 top up get added to my SIPP by the government.

Total added to my SIPP in that year
£10,000: £8,000 of my money + £2,000 top-up.

Year Two

Apply for a further tax rebate on the £8,000 contribution made in Year One. Let's assume that further rebate was £2,000 constituting a further 20% rebate because my marginal tax rate was 40% **AND I did pay a full 40% tax on that.**

Contribute the further £2,000 rebate to the SIPP. *This will only work if I get the tax rebate paid to me as cash rather than used to reduce my tax bill at the end of the financial year.*

The government automatically adds another £500 to my SIPP because of the £2,000 I've just paid into my SIPP.

IMPORTANT: I only get these top ups and rebates if I've paid this tax in the first place within the given time limits.

Next, I make my annual £8,000 contribution to my SIPP.
I watch the £2,000 top-up get added to my SIPP by the government.

Total added to my SIPP in that year

£2,000 higher-rate tax payer rebate, which I pay into my SIPP.
£500 basic-rate top up on that £2,000 contribution.
£8,000 of my personal contribution.
£2,000 basic-rate top up on that £8,000.
Total: £12,500 giving a running total after two years of £22,500

Year Three

I apply for a further tax rebate on the £12,500 I added to my SIPP in Year Two. I receive a tax rebate of £3,125.

Contribute the £3,125 to my SIPP.
The government automatically adds a top up of £781.

Make annual £8,000 contribution to my SIPP.
Watch the £2,000 top up get added to my SIPP by the government.

Total added to my SIPP in that year

£13,906, giving a running total of £36,406
And so on.

Regardless of your tax status, you should be adding money to your investments every month, even if it's just a few pounds. It's a good discipline and it makes a massive difference over time. This is the pound-cost averaging that Jasmine talked about in the foreword.

When 20% isn't 20%

The 20% figure is confusing. It is calculated as the 20% of the total amount that the government took in tax and is now giving back to you.

For example, if you received £8,000 after tax, the assumption is that the amount before tax was £10,000 and that you paid 20%

tax on that. Hence the "20%" top up is the £2,000 tax you paid before you were left with £8,000.

Turbo-charging example in numbers

	Contribution	Basic rate	Higher-rate tax payers only			
	£8,000 each year	+£2,000 top up	Rebate	Top up on rebate	Annual contribution	Running total
Year 1	£8,000	£10,000	£-	£-	£10,000	£10,000
Year 2	£8,000	£10,000	£2,000	£500	£12,500	£22,500
Year 3	£8,000	£10,000	£3,125	£781	£13,906	£36,406
Year 4	£8,000	£10,000	£3,477	£869	£14,346	£50,752
Year 5	£8,000	£10,000	£3,586	£897	£14,483	£65,235
Year 6	£8,000	£10,000	£3,621	£905	£14,526	£79,761
Year 7	£8,000	£10,000	£3,631	£908	£14,539	£94,300
Year 8	£8,000	£10,000	£3,635	£909	£14,544	£108,844
Year 9	£8,000	£10,000	£3,636	£909	£14,545	£123,389
Year 10	£8,000	£10,000	£3,636	£909	£14,545	£137,934
Totals	**£80,000**	**£100,000**				**£137,934**

This table provides numbers broken down over 10 years. Please bear in mind that this is an entirely hypothetical example used to show you the thinking behind how I claimed back tax payments and put them into my pension creating a virtuous circle.

Stay within the law

It's up to me, as the tax payer, to make sure that I stick to the tax rules within and beyond pension contributions. If I haven't paid it in tax, I can't claim it back.

Bottom line

Make the most of the tax rebate opportunities that you qualify for as the difference to your investment totals could be huge.

PART SEVEN

Using Their Research

20. My process
21. My portfolios, their research
22. How I select funds
23. Funds that passed my tests
24. My model portfolios
25. Why I have tiers
26. What's in my model portfolios
27. What if I already have some investments?
28. Moving up or down through the tiers
29. Annual review of my portfolio – "rebalancing"

20 My process

This is where we get into the mechanics and what works. For this, I'm going to talk about stuff I like from the perspective of an investor who doesn't want to think about investments. The intention is to set up a tax-efficient investment portfolio that looks after itself and is cheap to run.

The principles

Passive not active. I prefer passive funds or trackers. They're much cheaper and, in my opinion, much more likely to deliver a better return.

Diversified. I want some diversification across company shares, bonds and alternatives. The idea is that such a mix of investments should reduce the losses to the overall portfolio when bad things happen (viruses, dodgy politicians or bankers sticking their hands in, etc.)

Tax-efficient. I'm looking at both SIPPs and ISAs in equal measure because they've both served me well.

Why I avoid ready-made passive portfolios

A number of banks and investment companies offer read-made portfolios, some of which only include passive funds. I've studied quite a few of these and I don't like them for the following reasons:

- They involve some strange choices about how they allocate money when compared to the consensus of what assets investors should buy according to the 80+ risk-rated funds that I have researched and whose average view I try to copy

- They don't distinguish between different amounts of money that you might have to invest
- They don't allow for other investments that you might already have
- They tend to charge relatively high fees.

Bottom line

Passive funds, diversified, tax-efficient, low cost.

21 My portfolios, their research

How to decide what to invest in

This is the ultimate question when investing.

One solution would be to copy the asset allocations of a huge investment company that has spent hundreds of thousands of pounds on research and analysis.

The trouble with this approach is that each investment company has a slightly different set of allocations according to what their fund managers and research folk think.

So, instead of relying on one investment company, why not take the average asset allocation from a range of big, reputable companies with billions of pounds-worth of investments under management?

Their collective intelligence, my model portfolios

I have painstakingly gathered data from over 80 risk-rated funds and calculated the average allocation for me as a:

- **Lower-risk investor** - drawn from 26 lower-risk rated funds
- **Medium-risk investor** - drawn from 20 medium-risk rated funds
- **Higher-risk investor** - drawn from 35 higher-risk rated funds

By doing this, I've drawn on the collective research and analysis conducted by the investment companies and for which they charge their clients high fees.

Some surprises

No gold

Not one of them makes an allocation to gold. They prefer other alternatives to shares and bonds, such as real estate and absolute return funds (see glossary).

I like real estate funds as an alternative even though they sometimes will suspend trading when real estate prices move (usually downwards) quickly.

However, I hate absolute return funds because I've never seen one consistently deliver value for money over time. From what I've seen, they are an expensive folly.

Less cash

They make far lower allocations to cash than the ready-made portfolios do, averaging around 3% of the overall portfolio. That's still higher than I would want, but you do need enough cash to cover fees and charges.

My preference is to keep the cash allocation as low as possible but enough to ensure that all investment fees are covered i.e., no more than 2% of the overall portfolio. I don't need more cash on top of my cash buffer: I want my investments to work hard for me.

Self-serving

They love allocating to their own funds which, funnily enough, generate the highest fees for the respective bank or investment manager.

Actually, that wasn't a surprise, but it is worth mentioning.

The allocations

The main reason for allocating across shares and bonds is to diversify your investments. This diversification helps to make your overall investment portfolio less vulnerable to falls in a given type of investment.

In other words, you don't have all your eggs in one basket.

I plan to update the following allocations on a quarterly basis on my website, InvestWithoutBeingRippedOff.com, which is completely free to use.

The allocations shown below were the averages I calculated in early 2023. They probably won't change drastically, but it's worth checking the website just in case.

The steps I've taken for this book

This is here in case you were wondering how I conjured up the various numbers, funds, allocations and whatnot that appear later in the book.

Step One – sift through hundreds of investment funds

I researched hundreds (literally) of the largest investment funds and focused only on the ones that were risk-rated. That is, the ones that offer lower-, medium- and higher-risk rated portfolios to reflect different levels of risk for different investors.

Step Two – gather data on risk-rated funds only

I gathered all the allocation data publicly available for over 80 risk-rated funds; approximately 26 lower-risk, 20 medium-risk and 35 higher-risk.

Between them, these funds manage hundreds of billions (yes billions not millions) of pounds of invested money. As a result, the fees they charge mean that they have plenty of money to throw at research and analysis.

Based on that, and from all the research I've seen cross my desk, their allocations tend to be well thought through.

Step Three – Organise these data to provide average allocations

This took ages because I had to allow for all the different assets, funds, currencies, and more that the risk-rated funds allocated money to. By the end of it, I had a massive spreadsheet for each of the three risk-rated funds.

Step Four – Simplify the allocations for smaller investments

The final, averaged-out allocations covered 41 different asset classes.

While fund managers might wax lyrical about their fabulous research, best-in-class funds, and so on, I think that, for most normal human beings, 41 asset classes would demand a ridiculous amount of time to manage.

Also, bearing in mind the damning assessment of performance by the FCA, the fees you would pay on all those funds would be a complete waste of your hard-earned money.

Step Five – allowing for different amounts to invest

I've grouped those asset classes into broader categories which should be pretty obvious when you look at the pie charts. The less money there is to invest, the simpler the allocation.

This is purely to keep the fees down. As the amount to invest increases, the proportion of transaction and ongoing fees becomes less of an issue making me happier to include more funds and, therefore, incur more transaction fees.

For example, annual fees of £100 make a notable difference to someone with £1,000 to invest. That's much less important for someone with £10,000 to invest and even less important to someone with £50,000.

I've called these "tiers" of investment and they are as follows:

Tier 1 – £1,000 to £5,000
Tier 2 - £5,000 to £15,000
Tier 3 - £15,000 to £50,000
Tier 4 - £50,000 to £500,000
Tier 5 – More than £500,000

I've set up an investment portfolio using £10,000 of my own money, see Part Nine of this book. I've done this so that I can share with you the costs, performance and annual adjustments—the rebalancing.

Step Six – Sifting through thousands of funds to find low-cost passive funds

This also took a very long time. I had to trawl through thousands of funds to find low-cost passive funds that could be included in my low-cost portfolios. I cover this in Part 8 of this book.

Step Seven - Test investment platforms

Not as exhausting as Step Six but thoroughly time-consuming. I tested over 20 investment platforms that ordinary retail investors like you and me can use. I go into this in more detail in Part 8 of this book.

Step Eight - Set up actual investments

I've done this with my own money and am sharing the costs and performance on my website so that you can see examples of how it all works in practice.

Bottom line

I make free use of the results of the investment companies' and banks' expensive research and analysis.

22 How I select funds

I dragged my sorry backside through thousands and thousands of funds to find ones that are low-cost and which meet the asset-allocation criteria needed to build my low-cost portfolios.

These portfolios reflect the average allocations of all the banks, fund managers and investment companies offering risk-rated funds that I researched.

I welcome anyone who'd like to point out funds that I've missed. Generally speaking, they charge 0.15% or less. However, real estate and infrastructure funds tend to charge more.

I've included some funds that charge more (up to 0.20%) to make it possible to build my low-cost portfolios on as many platforms as possible.

Why include this list?

Simple - for transparency. I want to be completely open about what I've chosen and why.

What the table headings mean

Fund name

This speaks for itself.

OCF i.e., Ongoing Charges Figure

The OCF is what you're charged for putting money into a given fund. For example, if you have £1,000 invested in a fund and the OCF is 0.06%, you will be charged 0.06% of your £1,000 at the end of the year. 0.06% of £1,000 is 60p.

Yep, that's how little you can pay on some of these funds. Contrast that with the 1% or thereabouts that you can expect to pay on an active fund i.e., £10.

Low OCFs are essential

Think about an OCF of 1.00% for a second. It's 16 x the charge of 0.06% (my portfolios have a weighted overall OCF of between 0.05% and 0.08%).

An active fund might aim to outperform its benchmark by 2%. An OCF of 1.00% automatically wipes out half of it, and as we've gleaned from what the FCA has said, active funds tend not to hit their benchmarks, never mind outperform them.

On top of that, the benchmarks are all too often put together fairly arbitrarily (see the Glossary at the beginning of this book for what "arbitrary" equates to in this industry).

The truth about benchmarks?

The following chat more or less sums it up.

> **Fund manager:** Ah well, you see, the fact of the matter is, if you consider the seasonally adjusted benchmark, we performed much better than many had expected us to.
> **Investor:** But you missed the benchmark.
> **Fund manager:** Indeed. And rightly so under the circumstances.
> Investor: What were the circumstances?
> **Fund manager:** We had the wrong benchmark.
> **Investor:** Why?
> **Fund manager:** It had too much of the wrong investments in it.
> **Investor:** Why?
> **Fund manager:** Because the benchmark we came up with did better than we wanted it to.
> **Investor:** What are you going to do?
> Fund manager: Change the benchmark of course!
> **Investor:** Will that improve the performance of my investments?
> **Fund manager:** Oh yes.

Investor: Excellent. How much more will my investments grow by?
Fund manager: Your investments' growth? Oh, that won't change.
Investor: Then how can performance improve?
Fund manager: "Relative" performance my dear boy. With our new benchmark performing badly, the poor performance of your investments will look quite good. Well, less bad.
Investor: Relatively.
Fund manager: You're getting the idea.
Investor: How often do you change the benchmark?
Fund manager: Only when absolutely necessary.
Investor: When did you last change the benchmark?
Fund manager: When it was absolutely necessary.
Investor: Was it last year?
Fund manager: What's that? I say, my phone is ringing.
Investor: I can see it's turned off.
Fund manager: Hello Barbara...yes...very well. I'll be there as soon as I can.
Investor: The phone is off. There's no one there.
Fund manager: Must dash. Have an urgent lunch, er...emergency meeting. Pleasure doing business with you. Ciao.

Rip-Off Tip-Off

I take the benchmarks that investment funds use with a huge dose of salt. In my opinion, they can be confusing for the investor and convenient for the investment company. It's a bit like asking an MP about their recent, terrible by-election results.

In short, the OCF is hugely important and forms the backbone of my approach to investing. That's why I've listed the funds with the cheapest first. When I go to a platform to set up my low-cost portfolio, I look for the funds that I list below with the lowest OCF.

The International Securities Identification Numbering system (ISIN)

The ISIN is a unique number allocated to each fund. I've included it because it's by far the easiest way to find the precise fund that you're looking for.

Bear in mind that some platforms have 4,000 or more funds. Wading through loads of confusing and often indistinguishable names is a mug's game. I know, I've done it.

Why I don't look for sustainable, Environmental, Social and Governance (ESG) or impact funds

I'll keep an eye on these and would welcome fund managers pointing out the deep and verifiable green credentials of their funds. But, for now, I'll explain why I'm not convinced.

Standards without a standard

There are countless different standards, organisations, regulations and guidance forms competing for attention in this field at the moment (in 2023).

If you don't believe me, get a copy of the Chartered Financial Analyst (CFA) ESG Certificate book. It's a sodding great big tome that fogs around various elements of ethical investing.

Unfortunately, there's no clear framework yet that's won out over the others. As a result, loads of different fund management companies are adopting different standards and claiming to be green champions.

Greenwashing

I blow my nose at such champions because, having worked on the inside of several firms that purport to have green credentials, I have reached the sad conclusion that it's a large dose of box-ticking with little of substance to back it up in reality.

Where the funds that I like (low-cost, correct investment type) happen to have an ESG tilt to them, then fine and dandy. You'll see one or two of them in my list of low-cost funds.

The counter argument

A senior investment specialist was one of a number of people who proof-read this book. In response to my scepticism of sustainable funds, he said that "the challenge for investors is to navigate the ocean of false promises to find suitable investment opportunities". He adds that "some investors want to balance return and sustainability".

He's right. Therefore, I hereby appeal to funds to contact me if they are able to offer a fair balance between sustainability and fees that I can review and, potentially, share with my readers.

It's complicated

Finally, the sad truth of ethical, sustainable or green investing is that it's complicated.

For example, let's assume that you don't want to buy from a company based in a country with a terrible human rights record.

So far so easy. But...

> What about buying from a company that has a manufacturing base in said country?
>
> What about buying from a company that buys minerals from said country?

What about buying from a company that sells products or services to said country?

What if that country, while horrendous to humans, is the leader in sustainability, electric vehicles, clean air efficiency and so on?

How do you find out any of this?

Once you've found out you, as a retail investor, are entirely beholden to the layers of distance between you and where your money ultimately ends up.
Frankly, it's a proper nightmare.

I dearly hope that the world of sustainable and ethical investing will crystallise into a workable formula. But it's going to take time to work through the illusion, confusion and misrepresentation by players at all levels.

I'm focusing on funds that are low cost and very diversified. It's an approach that gives me what I consider to be about the best chance I have to do the right thing, inasmuch as I think that's possible.

In the meantime, here's a recent article published in the *Financial Times* that might help to explain my cynicism regarding so-called sustainable, green, impact or ESG investment funds:
https://www.ft.com/content/f1367ab4-ac6f-486d-8bd2-e7659448055d

Bottom line

I've done my best to provide a selection of funds that deliver very similar levels of risk and return to those provided by huge banks and investment companies, but at much lower costs.

23 Funds that passed my tests

Here is my list of low-cost passive funds and exchange-traded funds (ETFs) that (i) meet my criteria for covering the asset allocation I like while charging as little as possible, and (ii) which can be used on one of the four websites that do well in my reviews later in this book, namely Interactive Investor.

There are three other good websites as well, but there's only so much I can list in a table on these pages.

I provide the full list of all the funds I like in the Appendix. If you'd like to receive updates of when I've added or removed funds, you can sign up to my free, short, monthly newsletter at the website (address at the foot of this page).

From time to time, I'll update this list on my website as providers introduce more competitive fees, or as platforms introduce or drop funds from their respective offerings.

Any of the four websites I like could have been used here, so check the full review to see what I make of all the platforms before following up with your own decision making.

I'll come back to this when I start setting up investments in Part Nine of this book.

I provide the entire list of all funds I like at the time of writing in the Appendix.

So here we go with a list of funds; boring but very valuable.

Table 1 - Short-term bonds

Provider	Fund	OCF	ISIN
LGIM	L&G UK Gilt 0-5 Year UCITS EFT	0.06%	IE00BLRPQK69
Invesco	Invesco UK Gilt 1-5 Year UCITS ETF GBP Inc (GLT5)	0.06%	IE00BG0TQ445
BlackRock	iShares $ Treasury Bond 1-3yr UCITS ETF USD (Acc) B	0.07%	IE00B3VWN179
Credit Agricole	Lyxor UK Government Bond 0-5Y (DR) UCITS ETF - Dist-GBP (GIL5)	0.07%	LU1439943090
BlackRock	"iShares £ Ultrashort Bond UCITS ETF GBP (Dist)"	0.09%	IE00BCRY6441
Vanguard	USD Corporate 1-3 Year Bond UCITS ETF USD Accuimulation (VSCA)	0.09%	IE00BGYWSV06
ABRDN	abrdn Short Dated Sterling Corporate Bond Tracker Fund B Acc	0.10%	GB00BGMK1956
Vanguard	Sterling Short-Term Money Market Fund	0.12%	GB00BGB6GZ57
Vanguard	UK S/T Invm Grd Bd Indx £ Acc	0.12%	IE00B9M1BB17
LGIM	L&G Short Dated £ Corporate Bd Idx I Acc	0.14%	GB00BKGR3H21
ABRDN	abrdn Sterling Money Market Fund	0.15%	GB00B1C42332
SSGA	SPDR® Bloomberg 1-5 Year Gilt UCITS ETF (GLTS)	0.15%	IE00B6YX5K17
Vanguard	Global Short-Term Bond Index Fund	0.15%	IE00BH65QG55

Table 2 - UK government bonds

Provider	Fund	OCF	ISIN
Credit Agricole	Lyxor Core UK Government Bond (DR) UCITS ETF - Dist-GBP (GILS)	0.05%	LU1407892592
Invesco	Invesco UK Gilts UCITS ETF GBP Acc (GLTA)	0.06%	IE00BG0TQD32
BlackRock	iShares Core UK Gilts UCITS ETF	0.07%	IE00B1FZSB30
Vanguard	U.K. Gilt UCITS ETF (VGOV)	0.07%	IE00B42WWV65
LGIM	LEGAL & GENERAL ALL STOCKS GILT INDEX TRUST CLASS C - ACCUMULATION (GBP)	0.08%	GB00BG0QNW27
Fidelity	Fidelity Index UK Gilt Fund P GBP Acc	0.10%	GB00BMQ57G79
BlackRock	iShares UK Gilts All Stks Idx (UK) D Acc	0.11%	GB00B83HGR24
SSGA	SPDR® Bloomberg UK Gilt UCITS ETF (GLTY)	0.15%	IE00B3W74078
Vanguard	U.K. Government Bond Index Fund	0.12%	IE00B1S75374
HSBC	UK Gilt Index Fund	0.13%	GB00B80QG383
Fidelity	Fidelity UK Gilt W Acc	0.15%	GB0033144410

LGIM	L&G All Stocks Gilt Index I Acc	0.15%	GB00B8344798
SSGA	SPDR® Bloomberg UK Gilt UCITS ETF (GLTY)	0.15%	IE00B3W74078

Table 3 - Global government bonds

Provider	Fund	OCF	ISIN
Credit Agricole	Amundi Index Solutions - Amundi Prime Global Govies UCITS ETF DR (PRIG)	0.05%	LU1931975236
BlackRock	iShares Overseas Govt Bd Indx (UK) D Acc	0.11%	GB00B849C803
UBS	UBS (Lux) Fund Solutions - J.P. Morgan Global Government ESG Liquid Bond UCITS ETF, class (USD) A-acc	0.15%	LU1974693662
BlackRock	iShares Global Govt Bond UCITS ETF	0.20%	IE00BYZ28V50
BlackRock	iShares Global Govt Bond UCITS ETF	0.20%	IE00B3F81K65

Table 4 - Mixed bonds

Provider	Fund	OCF	ISIN
LGIM	L&G ESG GBP Corporate Bond UCITS ETF	0.09%	IE00BLRPQM83
BlackRock	iShares Core Global Aggregate Bond UCITS ETF GBP Hedged (Dist) (AGBP)	0.10%	IE00BF540Y54
Vanguard	Global Aggregate Bond UCITS ETF (VAGS)	0.10%	IE00BG47K971
SSGA	SPDR® Bloomberg Global Aggregate Bond UCITS ETF USD unhedged (GLBL)	0.10%	IE00B43QJJ40
Vanguard	U.K. Investment Grade Bond Index Fund	0.12%	IE00B1S74Q32
Vanguard	Global Bond Index Fund	0.15%	IE00B50W2R13

Table 5 - UK corporate bonds

Provider	Fund	OCF	ISIN
LGIM	L&G ESG GBP Corporate Bond UCITS ETF	0.09%	IE00BLRPQM83
Invesco	Invesco GBP Corporate Bond UCITS ETF Dist (IGCB)	0.10%	IE00BKW9SW28
Invesco	Invesco GBP Corporate Bond ESG UCITS ETF Dist (IGBE)	0.10%	IE00BKW9SV11
BlackRock	iShares Corporate Bond Index (UK) D Acc	0.11%	GB00B84DSW83
Vanguard	UK Invm Grd Bd Idx £ Acc	0.12%	IE00B1S74Q32
LGIM	"Legal & General Sterling Corporate Bond Index Fund "	0.14%	GB00B4M01C47
HSBC	Sterling Corporate Bond Index fund	0.15%	GB00BYV9WC94
UBS	UBS STERLING CORPORATE BOND INDEXED CLASS C - ACCUMULATION (GROSS GBP)	0.17%	GB00B95J1785
SSGA	SPDR® Bloomberg Sterling Corporate Bond UCITS ETF (UKCO)	0.20%	IE00B4694Z11

Table 6 - Global corporate bonds

Provider	Fund	OCF	ISIN
LGIM	L&G ESG GBP Corporate Bond UCITS ETF	0.09%	IE00BLRPQM83
BlackRock	ISHARES OVERSEAS CORPORATE BOND INDEX CLASS H - ACCUMULATION (GBP)	0.11%	GB00BPFJD529
BlackRock	iShares Overseas Government Bond Index Fund (UK) Class D Acc GBP	0.11%	GB00B849C803
BlackRock	iShares ESG Overseas Corporate Bond Index Fund (UK) Class D Acc GBP	0.10%	GB00B58YKH53

Invesco	Invesco USD Corporate Bond ESG UCITS ETF GBP Hedged (PUIP)	0.12%	IE00BJ06C481
HSBC	Sterling Corporate Bond Index Fund	0.15%	GB00BYV9WC94
Vanguard	Global Bond Index Fund	0.15%	IE00B50W2R13
Vanguard	Global Corporate Bond Index Fund	0.18%	IE00BDFB5M56
ABRDN	abrdn Global Corporate Bond Tracker Fund B Acc	0.18%	GB00BF473024
BlackRock	iShares Global Corp Bond UCITS ETF	0.20%	IE00BFM6TB42
BlackRock	iShares Global Corp Bond UCITS ETF USD (Dist) (CRPS)	0.20%	IE00B7J7TB45

Table 7 - UK all shares

Provider	Fund	OCF	ISIN
BlackRock	ISHARES UK EQUITY INDEX CLASS D - ACCUMULATION (GBP)	0.05%	GB00B7C44X99
Fidelity	FIDELITY INDEX UK CLASS P - ACCUMULATION (GBP)	0.06%	GB00BJS8SF95
HSBC	HSBC FTSE ALL SHARE INDEX CLASS C - ACCUMULATION (GBP)	0.06%	GB00B80QFX11
Vanguard	FTSE U.K. All Share Index Unit Trust	0.06%	GB00B3X7QG63
LGIM	LEGAL & GENERAL UK INDEX CLASS C - ACCUMULATION (GBP)	0.11%	GB00BG0QPJ30
Invesco	Invesco Markets II plc - Invesco FTSE All Share ESG Climate UCITS ETF (FASE)	0.12%	IE00BN7J5Z03
LGIM	L&G (N) Tracker Trust	0.15%	GB00B8386G47
ABRDN	ABRDN UK ALL SHARE TRACKER CLASS B - ACCUMULATION (GBP)	0.17%	GB00B76B9Y24
Aviva	"Aviva Investors UK Index Tracking Fund 2 GBP Inc"	0.20%	GB00B8XCGM21
SSGA	SPDR® FTSE UK All Share UCITS ETF Acc (FTAL)	0.20%	IE00B7452L46

Table 8 - Global shares

Provider	Fund	OCF	ISIN
Credit Agricole	Amundi Index Solutions - Amundi Prime Global UCITS ETF DR (PRIW)	0.05%	LU1931974692
LGIM	L&G Global Equity UCITS EFT	0.10%	IE00BFXR5S54
Fidelity	FIDELITY INDEX WORLD CLASS P - ACCUMULATION (GBP)	0.12%	GB00BJS8SJ34

SSGA	SPDR® MSCI World UCITS ETF	0.12%	IE00BFY0GT14
Vanguard	FTSE Developed World UCITS ETF (VHVG)	0.12%	IE00BK5BQV03
LGIM	L&G International Index I Acc	0.13%	GB00B2Q6HW61
LGIM	L&G Global Equity Index I Acc	0.13%	GB00B83LW328
HSBC	HSBC FTSE ALL WORLD INDEX CLASS C - ACCUMULATION (GBP)	0.13%	GB00BMJJJF91
Vanguard	FTSE Developed World ex-U.K. Equity Index Fund	0.14%	GB00B59G4Q73
HSBC	HSBC MSCI World UCITS ETF (HMWO)	0.15%	IE00B4X9L533
BlackRock	iShares MSCI ACWI UCITS ETF	0.20%	IE00B6R52259
BlackRock	iShares Core MSCI World UCITS ETF USD (Acc) (SWDA)	0.20%	IE00B4L5Y983

Table 9 - Alternatives

Provider	Fund	OCF	ISIN
BlackRock	"iShares Developed Real Estate Index Fund (IE) Class D GBP"	0.17%	GB00B5BFJG71
BlackRock	"iShares Developed Real Estate Index Fund (IE) Class D GBP"	0.24%	IE00BKPWSS48
HSBC	HSBC FTSE EPRA NAREIT Developed UCITS ETF (HPRO)	0.24%	IE00B5L01S80
LGIM	"Legal & General Global Infrastructure Index Fund "	0.30%	GB00BF0TZG22
SSGA	SPDR® Dow Jones Global Real Estate UCITS ETF (GBRE)	0.40%	IE00B8GF1M35
SSGA	SPDR® Morningstar Multi-Asset Global Infrastructure UCITS ETF (GIN)	0.40%	IE00BQWJFQ70
BlackRock	iShares UK Property UCITS ETF	0.40%	IE00B1TXLS18
BlackRock	iShares US Property Yield UCITS ETF	0.40%	IE00B1FZSF77

Table 10 - Gold funds

Provider	Fund	OCF	ISIN
BlackRock	iShares Physical Gold ETC (SGLN)	0.12%	IE00B4ND3602
Credit Agricole	Amundi Physical Gold ETC C (GLDA)	0.12%	FR0013416716
Invesco	Invesco Physical Gold ETC (SGLP)	0.12%	IE00B579F325

I don't include gold in any of the portfolios that I copy, but many investors feel comfortable with it, hence I've included some gold funds that are relatively cheap.

Bottom line

These are the funds that I like because they are diversified, backed by huge financial organisations and, best of all, they're cheap.

24 My model portfolios

Let's start with a quick recap of what I've done before I start selecting which portfolio is right for me.

I have:

- Cleared my bad debt
- Set up my cash buffer
- Completed the risk questionnaire and identified the appropriate level of risk for me
- Identified how much money I have available to invest.

If I happened to be a low-risk investor with £13,000 to invest, the model portfolio that I would consider most appropriate for me would be the Tier 2, Lower-Risk Model Portfolio.

If I were a higher-risk investor with £3,000 to invest, the model portfolio that I would consider most appropriate for me would be the Tier 1, Higher-Risk Model Portfolio.

Reminder: this is NOT ADVICE.

I am required by law to make this clear. All the following allocations are a reflection of what's available if you want to invest in a risk-rated fund. What's right for you will depend on your personal circumstances. There is no substitute for whole-of-market, independent financial advice and professional tax advice. And, yes, I am going to keep repeating that.

I call them model portfolios

This is because they are the portfolios that I'm trying to copy.

They reflect what I've found to be the average allocations made by lots of banks and investment houses for:

- Lower-risk rated portfolios
- Medium-risk rated portfolios
- Higher-risk rated portfolios

I went through the risk questionnaire to help me find the level risk appropriate for me.

No real-life investment portfolio will ever exactly match any model portfolio. I'm comfortable with that reality. My intention is to get as close as I can to the model portfolio that I consider to be most appropriate for me.

Bottom line

I find the right model portfolio to copy according to the appropriate risk level and the amount of money I have available to invest.

25 Why I have tiers

By "tiers", I mean "amounts of money to invest". For example, if I have between £1,000 and £5,000 to invest, I'd consider that Tier 1.

Here are all the tiers that I use:

- Tier 1: £1,000 to £5,000 to invest
- Tier 2: £5,000 to £15,000 to invest
- Tier 3: £15,000 to £50,000 to invest
- Tier 4: £50,000 to £500,000 to invest
- Tier 5: More than £500,000 to invest (wouldn't that be nice?!)

I use tiers of investment to try to keep the cost and benefit of including more funds, in proportion to the amount of money I have available to me to invest.

The less money I have to invest, the less I want to pay in transaction fees i.e., buying or selling funds.

To demonstrate what I mean, let's apply a Tier 4 Portfolio allocation to a Tier 1-sized portfolio.

Using a Tier 4 allocation for a Tier 1 Portfolio

Let's assume I'm a higher-risk investor with £3,000 to invest.

Let's also assume a cost per transaction of £8. This is similar to the fees incurred and demonstrated in the step-by-step investment examples in Part 9.

If I have an investment portfolio of £3,000 and buy eight different funds as is required in my higher-risk, Tier 4 Model Portfolio, I would have lost £64 in fees from my £3,000 investment portfolio straight away. I've just cost myself more than 2% of the portfolio's value.

Now let's compare using, firstly, an inappropriate model portfolio with an appropriate one.

Example 1 - Tier 4 allocations applied to a Tier 1 Portfolio

Day 1

I put £3,000 onto a platform of my choice.
I invest it in eight different funds costing 8 x £8 = £64.
I'm left with £3,000 - £64 = £2,936.

End of Year 1

Let's imagine that my overall portfolio has grown by 3%, a very respectable annual return.
This has raised my portfolio's overall value to £3,024.08.
I'm charged an OCF of around 0.08% equating to £2.42.
This leaves my portfolio at £3,021.66.

In this example, I would have made a gain on my original £3,000 of 0.72% over the year after fees.

Example 2 – Tier 1 allocations applied to a Tier 1 Portfolio

Day 1

I put £3,000 onto a platform of my choice.
I invest it in two different funds costing 2 x £8 = £16.
I'm left with £3,000 - £16 = £2,984.

End of Year 1

Again, let's imagine that my portfolio has grown by 3%, a very respectable annual return.
This has raised my portfolio's overall value to £3,073.52.
I'm charged an OCF of around 0.08% equating to £2.46.
This leaves my portfolio at £3,071.06.

In this example, I would have made a gain of 2.37% on my original £3,000 over the year after fees.

I'm going to keep reinvesting any gains. In other words, my gains will be compounded. An annual increase of 2.37% compounded, should get me to the next tier a good deal more quickly than a compounded annual gain of 0.72%.

Just to complete the picture, here's how much less important the transaction fees are in larger investment portfolios.

Example 3- Tier 4 allocations applied to Tier 4 Portfolio

Day 1

I put £50,000 onto a platform of my choice.
I invest it in eight different funds costing 8 x £8 = £64.
I'm left with £49,936.

End of Year 1

Once more, we imagine that my portfolio has grown by 3%, a very respectable annual return.
This has raised the portfolio's overall value to £51,434.08.
I'm charged an OCF of around 0.08% equating to £41.15.
This leaves my portfolio at £51,392.93.

In this example, I would have made a gain of 2.79% on my original £50,000

Bottom line

I try to balance the benefits and costs of having a broader set of investments in a portfolio.

26 What's in my portfolios

Tiers for souvenirs

Gawd bless Ken Dodd. I went to see him a couple of years before he died. Very glad I did. Like most people, I and my mates left at the half-time interval. Ken Dodd's idea of a show was getting on for five hours or more – I kid you not. We were exhausted after three hours.

The joke that stuck with me from that evening was this:

> "You know the UK tax people have a relatively new way of charging taxes? They spoke to me about it, obviously. They said, 'Have you heard of Self-Assessment?'.
> I said 'Heard of it? I invented it.'"

In case you're not aware, Ken Dodd had been fined for paying insufficient in tax on earnings.

If you're wondering why on Earth I'm blethering on about Ken Dodd, it's because he sang the song *Tears for Souvenirs* and "tiers" reminded me of that song. It's how my mind works.

Right. Investments. Here we go.

Less than £1,000 to invest

If I had less than £1,000 to invest, I'd set up a stocks and shares ISA and put money into that on a regular basis.

Once I'd reached at least £500, I'd buy one fund: if I were a low-risk investor, I would choose a low-cost passive fund tracking mixed bonds. If I were a medium- or higher-risk investor, it would be a low-cost passive fund tracking global shares.

Tier 1: Between £1,000 and £5,000 to invest

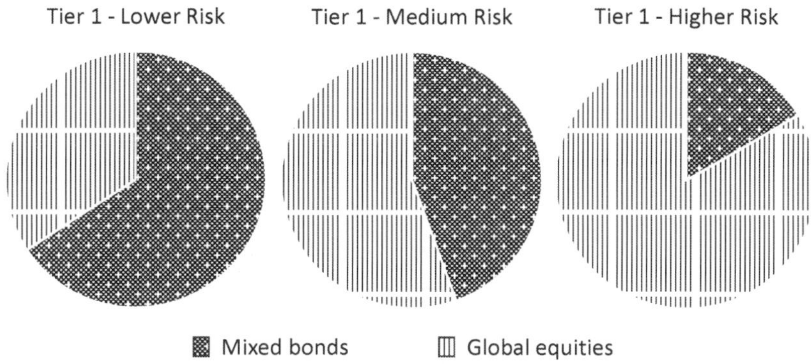

Risk	Cash*	Mixed Bonds	Global Shares
Lower	4% (at least £100)	64%	32%
Medium	4% (at least £100)	43%	53%
Higher	4% (at least £100)	18%	78%

**The allocation to cash is only there to cover the fees that come with investing. I'd leave that cash in my investment account so that I wouldn't have to sell investments in order to make sure there's enough in there to cover fees. £100 is usually enough to cover costs in Tier 1 when I used my low-cost funds and one of the platforms that did well in my research. However, SIPPs charge more, so I tend to leave around £200 in cash to cover the annual costs.*

Tier 2: Between £5,000 and £15,000 to invest

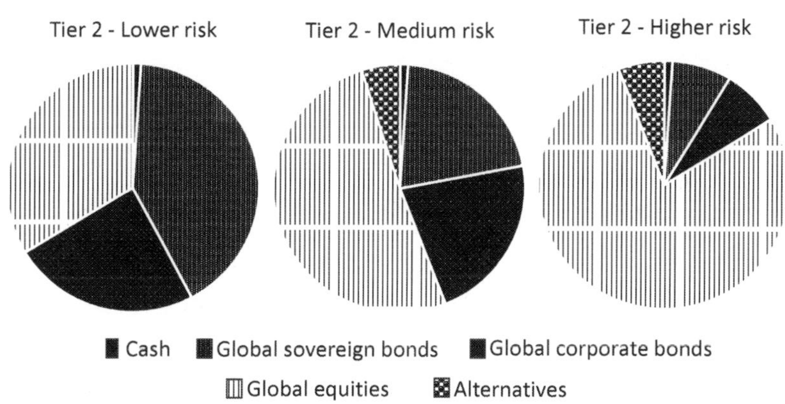

Risk	Cash*	Global Gov. Bonds	Global Corp. Bonds	Global Shares	Alternatives
Lower	1% (at least £100-£200)	41%	25%	33%	0%
Medium	1% (at least £100-£200)	21%	22%	51%	5%
Higher	1% (at least £100-£200)	8%	8%	78%	5%

**Same points as made under the Tier 1 table.*

Tier 3: Between £15,000 and £50,000 to invest

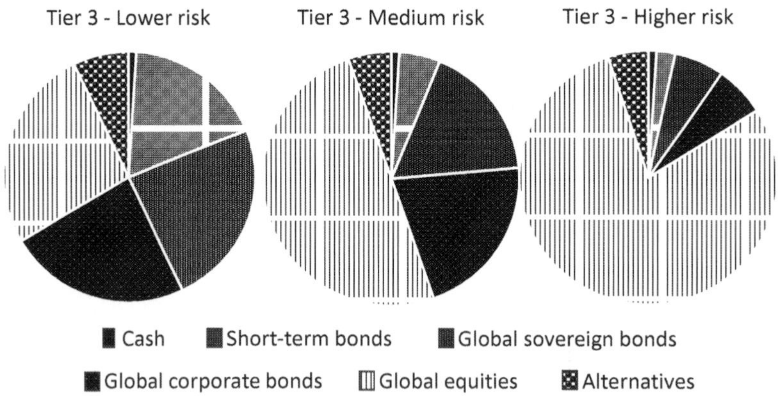

Risk	Cash	Short-term Bonds	Global Gov. Bonds	Global Corp. Bonds	Global Shares	Alternatives
Lower	1%	18%	24%	24%	26%	7%
Medium	1%	5%	17%	22%	50%	5%
Higher	1%	2%	6%	6%	80%	5%

Tier 4: Between £50,000 and £500,000 to invest

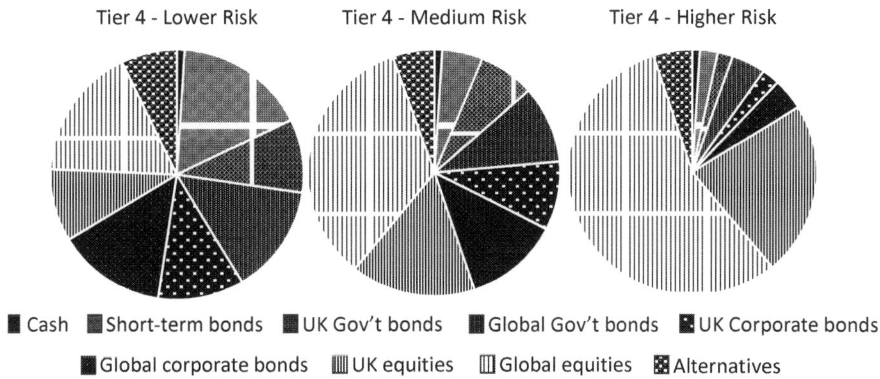

Risk	Cash	Short-term Bonds	UK Gov. Bonds	Global Gov. Bonds	UK Corp. Bonds	Global Corp. Bonds	UK Shares	Global Shares	Alts
Lower	1%	17%	10%	14%	11%	14%	9%	17%	7%
Medium	1%	5%	7%	10%	9%	12%	17%	34%	5%
Higher	1%	2%	2%	4%	2%	4%	23%	57%	5%

Tier 5: More than £500,000 to invest

This is the actual, detailed allocation that I derived from averaging out loads of allocations from banks and investment companies. It's the one that all the preceding tiers are based on.

The numbers go to two decimal points because, at this level, there is room for greater precision.

The pie-chart colours have been grouped for visual simplicity, but all 41 divisions are there with details provided in the subsequent tables.

Personally, I don't see the point of manually applying the minutiae of 41 different allocations when the categories by Tier 4 allocations take care of it to much the same effect.

But, in the unlikely event that you have a substantial sum to invest AND you want to get involved with the allocations (which can be fun if you're into it), then these allocations might be a point at which to start your thinking.

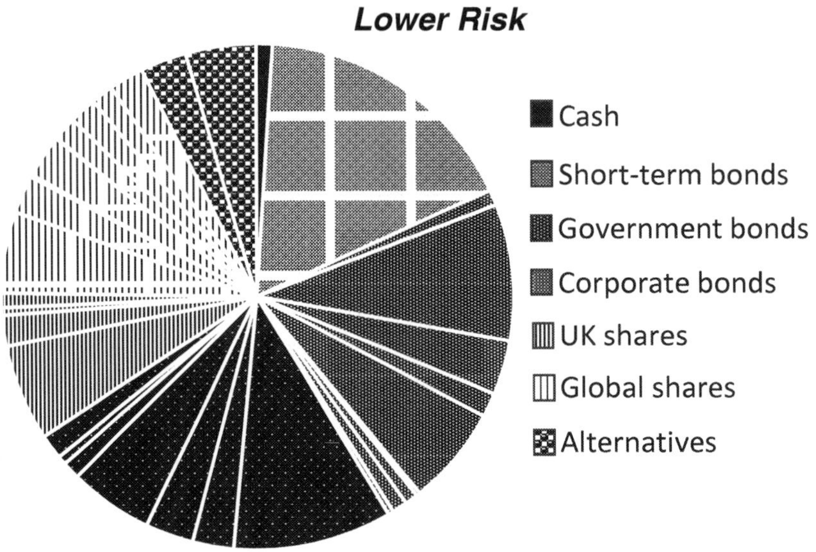

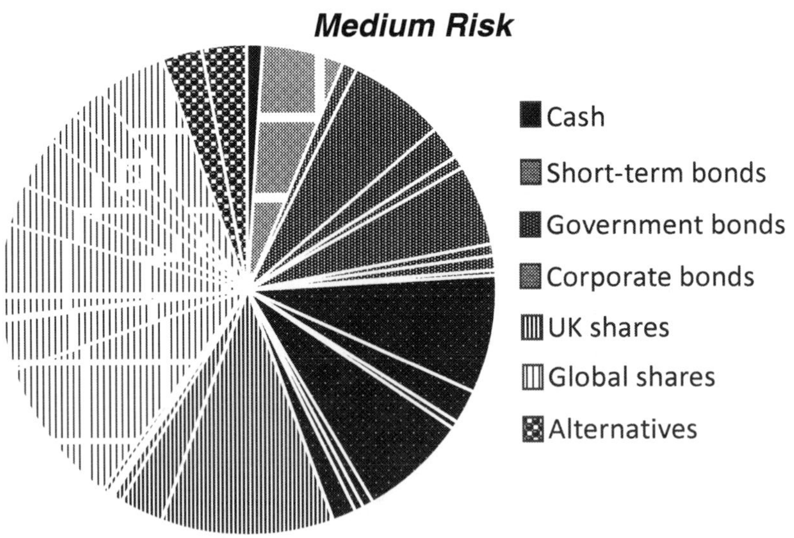

Higher Risk

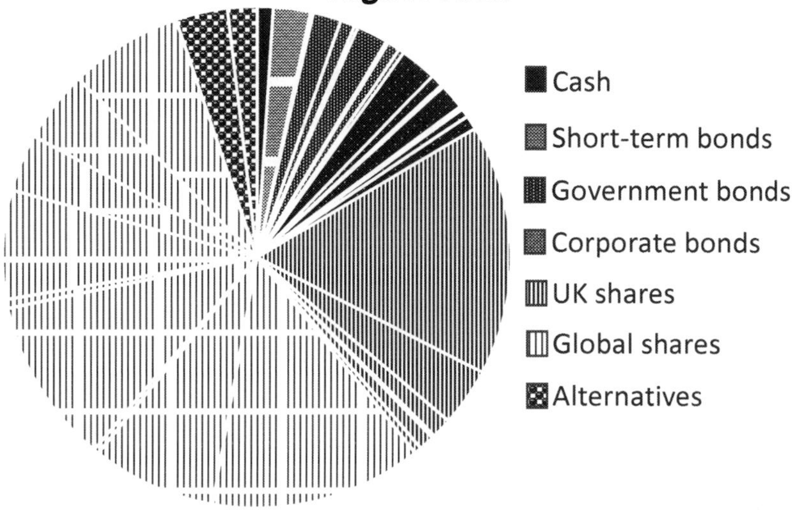

Cash and short-term bonds

Risk	Cash	Short-term Bonds
Lower	1.00%	16.76%
Medium	1.00%	5.20%
Higher	1.00%	2.32%

Government bonds

Risk	UK Index Linked	UK Nominal	US Nominal	Global Index Linked	Global Nominal
Lower	0.99%	8.51%	3.40%	1.52%	6.17%
Medium	0.95%	6.25%	2.17%	0.83%	5.20%
Higher	0.18%	1.76%	0.90%	0.23%	1.94%

Risk	Global Excluding Europe	Europe Nominal	Emerging Markets	High Yield
Lower	0.24%	0.79%	0.95%	0.33%
Medium	0.00%	0.74%	0.93%	0.34%
Higher	0.00%	0.14%	0.80%	0.33%

Corporate bonds

Risk	UK Nominal	US Nominal	Global Index Linked	Global Nominal	Europe Nominal	Emerging Markets	High Yield
Lower	9.78%	2.57%	2.95%	5.23%	1.09%	0.54%	1.55%
Medium	7.63%	2.19%	0.48%	6.94%	0.69%	0.56%	1.51%
Higher	2.29%	0.79%	0.16%	1.61%	0.20%	0.54%	0.88%

UK Shares

I've included "UK Shares" as a separate sector to demonstrate a domestic allocation for me as a UK-based investor.

A similar allocation could be considered for US Shares if I were a US-based investor.

This would also generate adjustments to allocations that, on these pages, are listed as "...Exclusing UK"; this could become "...Excluding US {or whichever is my country of domicile}".

Risk	All	Large	Medium	Small	Cyclical	Defensive
Lower	6.01%	1.94%	0.47%	0.00%	0.00%	0.90%
Medium	11.02%	2.80%	0.64%	0.19%	0.15%	0.37%
Higher	15.79%	3.68%	1.26%	0.17%	0.95%	0.45%

Other shares

Risk	US All	US Large	US Small	Global	Global Excluding UK
Lower	5.06%	2.39%	0.13%	2.69%	0.03%
Medium	9.64%	3.23%	0.23%	5.97%	2.67%
Higher	13.22%	7.75%	0.33%	10.43%	0.56%

Risk	Europe Excluding UK	Japan	Pacific Excluding Japan	Emerging Markets
Lower	1.51%	1.70%	1.40%	2.14%
Medium	3.38%	2.22%	2.18%	4.36%
Higher	6.88%	3.60%	4.49%	7.00%

Alternatives to stocks and bonds

Risk	Real Estate/Infrastructure	Other
Lower	2.83%	4.35%
Medium	2.58%	2.83%
Higher	3.26%	1.82%

Bottom line

I've worked really hard and drawn on my direct experience to construct risk-rated portfolios that emulate the collective research of some of the largest international banks and investment houses but for MUCH lower fees.

27 If I already have some investments

When setting up an investment portfolio, I would take into account any existing investments that I have in place. It's important to do this to make sure that I have the appropriate levels of risk and asset allocations across all my investments.

It means that I need to put a bit more thought into things before I set up new investments, but it's worth it.

Would I sell my existing investments?

Probably not. But I would want to make sure that I'm making full use of my tax-efficient investment opportunities (e.g., SIPPs and ISAs).

When you buy or sell investments you have to pay fees to do so. What's more, you might be liable to pay tax on any gains that those investments have made. Therefore, it's entirely possible that the best thing to do would be to leave those investments where they are and set up the new portfolio from scratch.

Assuming that leaving existing investments in place is the right thing to do, it can make sense to bear in mind what investments you have when setting up the new investments.

If I had an existing investment with a risk rating that's appropriate for me today, then I might leave it to do its thing and set up a new investment according to the risk rating and tier level that is appropriate for me.

When I might sell existing investments

If I were paying a high OCF and/or platform fees, I'd scrutinise the situation further to see if it would be worthwhile. This would depend on the various fees and tax liabilities I'd incur by doing so.

Rip-Off Tip-Off

With tax-free allowances falling, especially in the UK, it could be worth taking a small hit on tax to transfer money into something tax-efficient such as a SIPP or ISA. Professional advice could be useful at this point.

If the investments were in a pension or ISA account, I'd look into the costs of transferring to a cheaper/better platform.

Platforms hate it when you move your money to a cheaper alternative for obvious reasons. As a result, they'll put barriers in the way and might also charge excessive fees.

I'd have to look at what it would cost to make the transfer and decide if such a move would make enough of a saving in costs and an improvement in allocation over the investment time I have left before I need to dip into those investments.

In fact, I do have an existing pension from a former employer and it does not comply with my existing risk tolerance level (my risk tolerance is high, the fund's risk tolerance is medium). I didn't bother worrying about it when I set up my new investments. It wasn't worth the hassle for me.

But we're all in circumstances unique to our respective selves. Hence, it could be worth getting advice from an IFA with whole-of-market coverage.

If I were to consider existing investments when setting up new ones, here's how I'd go about it.

How might I adjust my new portfolio to allow for existing investments?

Let's assume that I have investments already set up that I've decided to leave where they are, untouched.

Here are some examples of how I might take into account those existing investments when setting up my low-cost portfolios on a platform that has done well in the review process that I conducted.

Example 1

Assume I have existing investments of 60% shares and 40% bonds.

Therefore, the existing investment of, say, £5,000 consists of £3,000 in shares and £2,000 in bonds.

Due to an inheritance, I now have an additional £5,000 to invest.

I decide to leave the existing £5,000 investment that's already invested (£3,000 in shares and £2,000 in bonds) where it is so that I don't incur any fees or tax liabilities by selling those investments.

Assume that my risk tolerance is for medium-risk rated investments.

I now have a total of £10,000 across all my investments (the invested £5,000 plus the recently inherited £5,000), which would put me in Tier 2.

The allocation in my Tier 2, Medium-Risk Model Portfolio as laid out in chapter 26 is £100 to £200 in cash, 21% global government bonds, 22% global corporate bonds, 50% shares, and 5% in alternatives.

Across the overall total of £10,000, that equates to £200 in cash, £2,100 global government bonds, £2,200 global corporate bonds, £5,000 in global shares, and £500 in alternatives.

The following table shows how I might allocate the additional money that I've received.

	Target allocations	**Total portfolio value**	**Already invested**	**How I'd allocate the additional £5,000**
Asset classes	Tier 2 Medium-Risk allocations	Allocations applied to £10,000	Existing allocations	New portfolio allocations
Cash	2%	£200	£0	£100
Global Gov. Bonds	21%	£2,100	£1,000	£1,100
Global Corp. Bonds	22%	£2,200	£1,000	£1,200
Global shares	50%	£5,000	£3,000	£2,100
Alternatives	5%	£500	£0	£500

These allocations to the new portfolio would bring the overall investment of £10,000 in line with the Tier 2, Medium-Risk Model Portfolio.

Any future, additional money added to the new portfolio can be added according to the Tier 2 medium-risk allocations (i.e., 2% cash, 21% global government bonds, 22% global corporate bonds, 50% global shares, 5% alternatives).

If the future additional amounts are fairly small, say £50 a month, then the investor could do any one of the following steps:

Allocate the additional contributions to cash and distribute the money into other asset classes once a year (this would be likely to incur the lowest costs because it would require the fewest trades).

OR

Month 1 - allocate the additional contribution to global government bonds.
Month 2 - allocate the additional contribution to global corporate bonds.
Months 3 and 4 - allocate the additional contributions to global shares; continue that sequence until the annual rebalancing.

OR

Allocate it all to global corporate bonds or global shares and rebalance once a year.

OR

Allocate it 50/50 across global corporate bonds and global shares (£25 each per month) and rebalance once a year.

Example 2

Let's assume that I have an existing investment of £10,000 allocated 80% (i.e., £8,000) to bonds and 20% (i.e., £2,000) to shares.

Let's also assume that I now have an additional £10,000 in cash to invest, perhaps through an inheritance. This gives me an overall total of £20,000. Finally, in this example, let's assume that I have a higher tolerance for risk in my investments.

£20,000 falls within Tier 3, which has the following allocations:

Risk	Cash	Short Term Bonds	Global Gov. bonds	Global Corp. Bonds	Global Shares	Alternatives
Lower	1%	18%	24%	24%	26%	7%
Medium	1%	5%	17%	22%	50%	5%
Higher	**1%**	**2%**	**6%**	**6%**	**80%**	**5%**

The Higher-Risk Portfolio allocates just 14% to bonds (2% short-term + 6% global government + 6% global corporate = 14%).

14% of £20,000 = 0.14 x £20,000 = £2,800.

I already have £8,000 allocated to bonds, which is much higher than the portfolio I've decided is right for me, the Tier 3, Higher-Risk Model Portfolio.

Option 1 - simple but might cost a bit more

I could sell the existing investments which would give me a total of £20,000 in cash, and allocate it according to the Tier 3, Higher-Risk Model Portfolio i.e., 1% cash, 2% short-term bonds, 6% global government bonds, 6% global corporate bonds, 80% global shares and 5% alternatives.

This would be a simple way of doing things and would set me up nicely for the future, but it might incur more in costs and tax liabilities.

If the investments were not in a tax-efficient investment structure such as a SIPP or an ISA, I would still consider this option because the tax liability might be low and I'd want to set myself up for a long-term investment timescale with as much of my investments as possible in a SIPP or ISA.

Speaking for myself, my preference is for a simple life. Therefore, this would be my way of doing things especially with this relatively low amount of money to invest.

If you're not sure, as always, professional advice is worth considering from an IFA.

Option 2 - more complex

Alternatively, I could decide to keep the existing investments where they are to avoid fees, tax liabilities and hassle.

If I really wanted to, I could examine what the bonds are and come up with a detailed assessment of the bonds I have and the bonds I want to invest in. That's beyond the scope of this book as it requires a level of investment and allocation understanding that you'd probably be better off getting from an IFA.

To keep things a little simpler in this more complex example, I'm not going to worry too much about how much of that is short-term, government, corporate, global and so on.

What I will focus on is the fact that I have too much money allocated to bonds across my overall investments of £20,000.

In my new portfolio (the additional £10,000 in cash), I will allocate the £10,000 to everything except bonds.

As we've seen, the allocations in the Tier 3, Higher-Risk Model Portfolio are 1% cash, 2% short-term bonds, 6% global government bonds, 6% global corporate bonds, 80% global shares and 5% alternatives.

For the entire £20,000 across all the money I have available to invest, that equates to:

- **Cash:** 1% of £20,000 = 0.01 x £20,000 = £200
- **Short-term bonds:** 2% of £20,000 = 0.02 x £20,000 = £400

- **Global government bonds:** 6% of £20,000 = 0.06 x £20,000 = £1,200
- **Global corporate bonds:** 6% of £20,000 = 0.06 x £20,000 = £1,200
- **Global shares:** 80% of £20,000 = 0.80 x £20,000 = £16,000
- **Alternatives:** 5% of £20,000 = 0.05 x £20,000 = £1,000

Next step

I bring the allocation to cash up to £200 (1% of the overall £20,000), and allocate the rest to global shares.

Over time, as I continue to add to my investments, I would only allocate additional money to global shares until that allocation reaches 80% of my overall portfolio.

This would take a long time and wouldn't happen until I had a total investment portfolio of at least £57,000; another reason why I'd be much more likely to keep things simple by selling the bonds and starting again.

Getting close to retirement

If I were getting closer to retirement, I might want to reduce the amount of risk in my overall investments.

The reason for this is that, once I've retired, I'm no longer earning money. I need to live off the investments and need them to be less vulnerable to the ups and downs of the financial markets.

If you are getting close to retirement then it would almost certainly make sense for you to pay for advice from an IFA. The state pension isn't sufficient to live off, so you can't afford to make the wrong decisions.

Bottom line

I want to get things right from the get-go. Hence I'd use the appropriate level of risk and invest in tax-efficient wrappers. The better the set up, the less I have to worry about later on.

28 Moving through the tiers

Rip-Off Tip-Off

If you are not at this stage yet, don't feel you have to read it. It takes a bit of concentration and will make far more sense when you are experiencing it for yourself.

What would I do if my overall investments moved from one tier to another?

I've tried to make it simple, but you'll need to bear with me as I go through it. Hang in there soldier.

Going down a tier

Investments can, and absolutely will, go down as well as up.

Once I've invested wisely with the appropriate level of risk and diversification for me, I don't focus on the overall value of my investment portfolio going up or down. I accept that it will fluctuate and that worrying about it will just get me stressed.

My focus is on adding to my investments as much and as often as possible.

If my investment portfolio falls in value taking it from, say, Tier 3 to Tier 2, it doesn't bother me.

This is because the tiers I have are designed to keep costs proportionate to the size of my investment. If I already have a Tier 3 allocation in place, then most of the transaction costs have already been incurred. I don't want to sell and buy funds again and incur transaction costs just because of short-term fluctuations in the market.

I'd just keep using the Tier 3 allocations (or whichever tier I'm in) and rebalance once a year. I cover rebalancing in more detail in chapter 29.

Prioritise the cash buffer

There might be need for me to find a big chunk of money to deal with an unforeseen issue. My six-month buffer is designed for precisely this purpose. It should deal with the majority of such events.

If you find yourself in a situation where you've used your cash buffer but still need to raid your investments to cover an expense of some sort, here are some actions to consider:

- Am I expecting to receive some money soon that could cover the upcoming expense?
- Can I withdraw a part of the investment and add it back later?
- Would I incur fees for the partial withdrawal and repayment?
- Could I take money from an ISA or GIA first and pay it back later?

If none of these seems sensible or possible, the next step would be to contact one of the free financial, objective resources listed in the Resources section at the back of the book.

Let's suppose something happened that meant I had to dip into the cash buffer.

I would stop adding more money to my investments and, instead, channel those payments into my cash buffer until it was back up to its full value again. Only then would I return to adding money into my investments.

> ***Rip-Off Tip-Off***
>
> Remember, if you've had to dip into your cash buffer, you've succeeded. It might not feel like it, but you've used the cash buffer for precisely the sort of purpose for which you were smart enough to set it up.

Going up a tier

Over time, as you keep adding to your investments, you should see them increase in overall value. With luck, you'll face the happy challenge of moving up through the investment tiers that I've described.

You don't have to change anything if you don't want to

You don't actually have to change anything. If you're happy with how things are going, have peace of mind and are growing your investments nicely, you can just keep on going as you are.

However, if my portfolio grew into a higher tier and I wanted to emulate what I found to be the collective outlook and allocation of the banks and investment houses that I researched, the following is how I might go about it.

Tier 1 to Tier 2

Firstly, I'd give myself a BIG pat on the back. I've just achieved what I consider to be the hardest part of investing - establishing the right habits and sticking with them.

Rip-Off Tip-Off

One of my trustworthy advisor friends read the "pat on the back" bit and said "Love this! Can't be overstated enough. People need to recognise their achievements".

Some small adjustments would make my investments more precisely reflect what the experts, with all their research and analysis, think. Here are those adjustments:

- Cash £100 to £200. I'd make sure my cash allocation is enough to cover the fees I'll have to pay each year. I don't fret if the numbers aren't precisely in line with the allocation I'm copying; it doesn't have to be exactly 1% in cash. It'll probably be slightly more as will become clear in the step-by-step examples in Part 9 of this book.

- Change the bond allocation. This will incur some transaction costs but it's worth it. I'd sell the mixed bonds allocation and put that money towards the Tier 2 allocation of global government bonds and global corporate bonds.

- (Medium- and Higher-Risk only) Additional money that was being allocated to global equities would be allocated to alternatives until alternatives reached 5% of my overall investments. Once alternatives have reached 5% of my overall investments, I'd be able to allocate between global shares and alternatives according to my risk profile.

- Additional money allocated according to Tier 2 allocations. Having completed the preceding three points, my investment portfolio would now reflect the Tier 2, Model Portfolio that I'm copying. From this point on, I can allocate additional money that

I invest across the investment portfolio in line with the allocations in the appropriate Tier 2 Model Portfolio.

Tier 2 to Tier 3

At this tier, short-term bonds are introduced.

They are included to help offset short-term fluctuations in market prices caused by, say, idiots invading their neighbouring countries, viruses spreading around the world and stupid political decisions.

I don't include short-term bond allocations at lower tiers because of the transaction costs. However, at this tier, I think the extra costs are a small enough proportion of the overall portfolio to be worthwhile.

The overall amount of money I have invested is a bit more significant now. So let's address the potential changes for each risk-rated, tier 3 portfolio in turn.

Lower-Risk portfolio

- Cash stays at £100 to £200.
- New allocation to short-term bonds. Short-term bonds have a fairly predictable future in which their prices don't change much. The more risk-averse an investor is, the more likely they are to include short-term bonds in their portfolio. Like cash, short-term bonds don't tend to rise and fall as much as other bonds and company shares.
- New allocation to alternatives. I'd be tempted to move money out of global equity and into alternatives at this tier level for the same reasons as mentioned in the preceding paragraph.

Medium-Risk portfolio

- Cash stays at £100 to £200.
- New allocation to short-term bonds. If I were making relatively modest contributions on a monthly basis (less than £200) then I'd be inclined to move some money out of global

government bonds and into short-term bonds to match the tier allocation.

Higher-Risk portfolio

There's hardly any change to the overall allocations in my model portfolios here. I'd just carry on as before and only make adjustments during my annual rebalancing.

Tier 3 to Tier 4

If I were starting with £50,000 or more, I would start with this allocation. But I might not bother changing my allocation if my investments grew from Tier 3 to Tier 4.

The extra precision would bring my investments more closely in line with what the investment industry as a whole tends to foresee as a good allocation strategy. However, it would take more time and incur some extra transaction costs, so I'd only change allocations if I enjoy the process.

I daresay there are plenty of people in the financial services industry who would huff and puff about the value of risk management of assets and whatnot. They're the same people who charge lots of money and then fail to meet their own targets (according to the FCA), hence I take anything they say with a good deal of salt.

Tier 5

In all my years in the financial industry providing performance reports, analysis and commentary, I have never seen the value to the investor of this detailed level of asset allocation. Will allocating money across 41 asset classes justify the extra fees and hassle? Not from what I've seen.

Nevertheless, I have brought together the low-cost funds and means of setting up a Tier 5 Model Portfolio for two reasons:
It shows you the ultimate model portfolio upon which all the lower tiers are based

If you really enjoy this sort of thing and have the money and time to do it, you might want to get this deeply involved in the mechanics of "running money" as it's referred to in the industry.

Bottom line

The more I have to invest, the more precise I'll be with my allocations…up to a point.

29 Annual review, "rebalancing"

Rebalancing is adjusting the allocations within my portfolio to make sure that they are still in line with my model portfolios.

I want to match the appropriate model portfolio because it represents what I found to be the average allocation made by massive banks and investment firms who've put loads of research and analysis into this.

How often do I rebalance?

This is something I do annually. Some people with large investment portfolios (more than £50,000) might prefer to do this more often but I think that just incurs fees and is too much of a hassle.

Generally speaking, I would rebalance once a year if my portfolio has deviated by 5% or more from the Model Portfolio that I'm following.

For example, if the Model Portfolio allocates 1% in cash, 45% in mixed bonds and 54% in global shares but my portfolio has moved to 2% in cash, 41% in mixed bonds and 57% in global shares, then I'd be inclined to sell 3% of the global shares and buy 4%-worth of mixed bonds. This would also reduce the cash holding to 1%.

If the deviation from thc Model Portfolio is really small, I might just add money to one asset class to bring my portfolio back in line with the Model Portfolio.

For example, if the most appropriate Model Portfolio for me was the Medium-Risk Tier 1 Model Portfolio, it would have target allocations of £100 to £200 in cash, 45% in mixed bonds and 54% in global shares.

But if my actual portfolio worked out at, say, £200 in cash, 44% mixed bonds and 55% global shares, then I could just keep adding to the mixed bonds pot until it more or less reached 45% of the overall investment portfolio.

Change in personal circumstances

If something happened to me that made my appetite for risk change, then I would almost certainly change my investment allocations to reflect my new situation.

Rip-Off Tip-Off

It's a good idea to retake the risk assessment questionnaire in chapter 16 of this book every three to four years. Things change and your answers might indicate a different appetite for risk (lower or higher).

For example, if I realised that I had become more (or less) comfortable with risk, then I would retake the risk assessment questionnaire.

If these more recent results indicated that my appetite for risk had changed, I would reallocate my investments to match the model portfolio that most closely reflected my new appetite for risk. The process would be the same as that used when rebalancing my portfolio.

When I might start to rebalance

Let's suppose that I set up a Tier 2, Medium-Risk portfolio one year ago with £10,000. When I set it up, I allocated the money to match the Tier 2, Medium-Risk Model Portfolio’s allocations.

I then spend a year not thinking about my investments but, rather, getting on with my life and letting the investments take care of themselves. Very sensible. After a year, it’s time to take a look at my investments and see if I need to make any adjustments.

Ignore the overall value

I’m not concerned with whether the overall portfolio has grown or fallen in value. I know that, having set up the investments properly in the first place, their best chance of growing is if I leave them alone and not fiddle with them. Fiddling with them costs me money and is likely to leave me worried about the short-term price movements of bonds and shares.

Focus on the allocations

I am concerned with what the allocations are to the different asset classes. I’ll update the model portfolios on the website.

For the purpose of explaining rebalancing here, let’s assume that the model portfolio hasn’t changed.

The charts and table below show the model portfolio’s allocations on the left and what my portfolio’s allocations are after a year of being left alone to do their thing.

	Cash	Global Gov. Bonds	Global Corp. Bonds	Global Shares	Alternatives
Model portfolio	*1%*	*21%*	*22%*	*51%*	*5%*
My portfolio	**1%**	**17%**	**24%**	**54%**	**4%**
My current allocation is...	Balanced	4% too low	2% too high	3% too high	1% too low

Actions I need to take

I can see the following:

- Cash has remained at roughly 1%, so I don't need to do anything about that - it matches or "balances" with the model portfolio's allocation to cash

- Global government bonds account for 17% of the overall portfolio. They might have fallen in value or grown at a slower speed than other assets; it makes no difference. What matters is that I need to increas e the allocation to global government bonds by four percentage points so that the allocation reaches 21% of my overall portfolio.

- Global corporate bonds account for 24% of the overall portfolio. I need to reduce that to 22%.

- Global equity has risen to 54%, so I need to reduce that to 51%.

- Alternatives have dropped to 4%. That needs to be raised to 5%.

The allocations here are still fairly close to the model portfolio's allocations. I could just leave it alone for another year and only rebalance if something goes more than 5% away from the model allocations.

But it's only once a year and I want to keep in line with the Model Portfolio because things can change suddenly and I don't want things to go too far off course.

Therefore, in this instance, I would move some money from global corporate bonds into global government bonds, and I'd move some money from global equity into both global government bonds and into alternatives.

The numbers

Simple example

Let's assume that the overall portfolio hasn't grown in value and remains at exactly £10,000.

1% of £10,000 = £100 (£10,000 x 0.01).

Therefore, in this example, I need to do the following:

- Move 2% i.e., £200, out of global corporate bonds and into global government bonds
- Move 3% i.e., £300, out of global equity and
  - ◊ put £200 of that into global government bonds
  - ◊ put the remaining £100 into alternatives.

More realistic example

The numbers are never conveniently round. Let's take an example in which I have, say, £13,754. 1% of £13,754 = £137.54 (£13,754 x 0.01).

Therefore, in this example, I need to do the following:

- Move 2% i.e., £275.08, out of global corporate bonds and into global government bonds
- Move 3% i.e., £412.62, out of global equity and
  - ◊ put £275.08 of that into global government bonds
  - ◊ put the remaining £137.54 into alternatives.

The actual numbers would not be this precise. When you invest in a fund you buy "units" in a fund. The cost of each unit changes all the time and it's rarely a nice round number.

For example, I might have £137.54 with which to buy units in my preferred alternatives fund but each unit might cost, say, £5.37.

That would allow me to buy 25 units of the alternative fund for a total value of £5.37 x 25 = £134.25. This would leave £3.29 unspent and sitting in my cash allocation, which is fine.

You'll see this in practice in the step-by-step examples in Part 9 of this book.

I'd aim to take, say:

- Between £270 and £280 out of global corporate bonds and put it into global government bonds.
- Between £410 and £420 out of global equity and
  - ◊ put between £270 and £280 of that into global government bonds
  - ◊ put as much as whatever's left as I can into alternatives.

Bottom line

I do this once a year to keep an eye on things. It should take an hour, maybe two.

PART EIGHT

Investment Websites

30 Choosing an investment website

So far, I have:

- Cleared my "bad" debt
- Set up a cash buffer
- Completed the risk questionnaire and know which level of risk is appropriate for me (lower, medium or higher)
- Confirmed how much money I have available to invest
- Identified the model portfolio that I consider to be most appropriate for me.

What do I do next?

I need to select a website that will enable me to set up my investment portfolio.

Investment websites are also referred to as "platforms"

I've reviewed around 25 of them and, trust me, they vary enormously in how good or bad they are.

I started with the platforms that *Which?* magazine and its website have reviewed. I also considered a few more that came up a lot in my research.

The *Which?* review is good as far as it goes. But the folk there are not investment specialists and nor do they claim to be. Their reviews don't address the fees incurred with specific investments as this is beyond their remit. For me, this is the most important factor, hence my reviews differ from those of *Which?*

Anyhow, my review of platforms covers everything relating to my concept of "How to invest without being ripped off".

How I scored the different platforms

I assessed each platform according to criteria specified below. Sign up to my monthly newsletter on the website for updates.

Fund range – 50% of the overall score

This is much the most important factor as far as I'm concerned.

If the platform doesn't offer sufficient low-cost funds for me to build my investment portfolio then that platform is of no use to me.

To be clear, the platform doesn't necessarily have to have huge numbers of funds to get a good score. It has to offer enough of my 110 or so qualifying low-cost funds for me to be able to build my low-cost portfolios.

For example, let's take Fidelity and FreeTrade. The latter made it onto my shortlist of platforms to consider using, while the former did not despite Fidelity offering far more funds than FreeTrade does.

Fidelity offers around 4,000 funds. The vast majority of these are of no use to my portfolios because they either don't cover the asset classes I want, or they're too expensive.

By contrast, FreeTrade offers around 700 funds but manages to cover most of the needs of my portfolios, albeit with a couple of limited selections.

The actual score achieved reflects the percentage of my qualifying funds that the platform offers. For example, if the fund offers 56 of my roughly 110 funds (i.e., half of my qualifying funds), it gets a score of 50%.

There is an obvious weakness in this scoring: if a platform offers half of the funds on my entire list but only offers bond funds, then that platform is not much use. However, while one or two platforms had weak spots, none of them was quite that tragic.

Where there were blind spots, I mention them in the accompanying notes and included it in my judgment as to the final rating I awarded each platform.

Platforms that do not offer individual funds are of no use to me. Hence, I rated them as "did not qualify".

Tax-efficient offerings - 30% of score

ISA offered - 15% of the overall platform score
SIPP offered - 15% of the overall platform score

The next most important fact for me is whether or not I can have a tax-efficient investment account i.e., either a SIPP or ISA. (I explain what these are and their respective pros and cons in Part 6).

The point being that I don't want to have to pay tax on any money my investments make if I can possibly avoid it.

As far as my scoring is concerned, the platform either does or doesn't offer ISAs or SIPPs. They were awarded 100% if they did offer an ISA or SIPP and 0% if they did not.

Low platform fees £0-£50k - 12% of score

I've largely focused on portfolios whose total value is up to £50,000 to keep things simple. Things get complicated quickly with platform fees because they all have different fee structures and rates, and some of them make it difficult to work out what you're actually going to pay.

I calculated it by estimating what the costs would be on each platform allowing for a reasonable number of trades each year (e.g., one trade per investment type/asset class in each portfolio per year).

I identified the platform charging the highest fee and gave it the lowest score of 0%. The other platforms were awarded scores according to how much lower than that their fees were.

This only contributes 12% to the overall platform score because it's less important than the preceding factors.

Ease of use - 8% of the overall platform score

This is more of a "nice-to-have" than an essential.

The best-performing platform on this score for me was Halifax. It was a joy to use; simple, responsive, and easy to follow. Unfortunately, this wasn't enough for it to earn it a place in my top selection of platforms because it didn't score highly enough in the preceding factors.

As a side note, I did not consider the existence of mobile phone apps for the respective platforms for the simple reason that I want to forget about the investments. Having an app simply invites repeated viewings and worry about investments.

Calculating the overall scores

I rated each platform according to the preceding factors and then applied the weighting to each factor. I then added them up to generate a final score.

Here are two examples of how this worked in practice.

Example 1 – Fidelity

Criterion	Score	Weighting	Score x Weighting
Range of funds	79%	50%	= 79% x 50% = **39.5%**
ISA offered	100% (i.e., offered)	15%	= 100% x 15% = **15%**
SIPP offered	100% (i.e., offered)	15%	= 100% x 15% = **15%**
Platform fees	34%	12%	= 34% x 12% = **4.1%**
Ease of use	70%	8%	= 70% x 8% = **5.6%**
Total			**79.2%**

Example 2 – Trading 212

Criterion	Score	Weighting	Score x Weighting
Range of funds	26%	50%	= 26% x 50% = **13%**
ISA offered	100%	15%	= 100% x 15% = **15%**
SIPP offered	0% (not offered)	15%	= 0% x 15% = **0%**
Platform fees	0% (not offered)	12%	= 0% x 12% = **0%**
Ease of use	80%	8%	= 80% x 8% = **6.4%**
Total			**34.4%**

Notes

This is the part in which I add comments on why platforms scored the way they did. It also allows me to include background to the bald numbers which, on their own, don't tell the whole story.

For example, Barclays and Halifax earned high scores but did not make it onto my "Yes" list for reasons I explain in the accompanying notes.

Which ones would I consider using?

This is my conclusion after considering all the scores and any comments I made while reviewing the platforms.

I've broken this down to:

> **Yes** - I would definitely consider using this platform and moving money to it from other platforms.
>
> **Maybe** - I would consider staying with this platform but there would be others I'd sooner start new accounts with.
>
> **No** - I would not consider using this platform. In fact, I would seriously consider moving my money off this platform and onto one that scored more highly in my analysis.
>
> **DNQ** – this platform does not qualify (DNQ) as it doesn't offer individual funds.

Bottom line

An appropriate range of low-cost funds is the most important factor in my review of investment platforms.

31 My reviews of websites

As mentioned, I've grouped these into "Yes", "Maybe" and "No". They are in no particular order within those groups.

Category: Yes

I would happily use these platforms

I would happily set up new accounts or transfer existing accounts into any of these platforms, which earn a Yes from me.

The Yes platforms:

Interactive Investor
FreeTrade
InvestEngine
AJ Bell

Interactive Investor

Overall Score	**72%**
Fund range	77%
ISA offered	Yes
SIPP offered	Yes
Low platform fees	14%
Ease of use	20%

The excellent selection of funds is let down a tiny bit by the website and relatively high platform fees for sub-£50,000 portfolios. But there is a cash-back payment; I got £100 which effectively slashed the platform fees for the first year.

I ignored the expensive ready-made portfolios and looked, instead, for the individual passive funds by searching by ISINs.

To search by ISIN, you have to set up an account, login and use the different search functions under one of the following: fund, investment trust, or ETFs. I couldn't do a one-off search for an ISIN under all offerings.

The range of passive funds is plenty good enough for my low-cost portfolios and the process of setting up a £10,000 SIPP was a doddle (unlike some of the other sites I tested).

FreeTrade

Overall Score	**60%**
Fund range	28%
ISA offered	Yes
SIPP offered	Yes
Low platform fees	72%
Ease of use	90%

FreeTrade offers very low platform fees and offers sufficient fund choice for me to build my Model Portfolios, albeit with a limited choice among global bonds and UK shares.

The website is easy to use with a search function that seems to work. Also, you can view FreeTrade's entire list of funds, shares and bonds as a spreadsheet, which you can download if you want. It's a searchable list and is updated on a regular basis.

A further note is warranted for FreeTrade's very low platform fees. Vanguard's platform fees are a tiny bit lower for portfolios under £50,000. After that, FreeTrade leaves the rest in the dust in this regard, for the simple reason that it continues to charge a tiny fixed annual fee of £36 (at the time of writing). Everyone else charges a percentage of the portfolio which grows as the portfolio grows.

InvestEngine

Overall Score	**43%**
Fund range	32%
ISA offered	Yes
SIPP offered	Yes
Low platform fees	65%
Ease of use	50%

This platform offers lowish platform fees and sufficient low-cost funds to build my low-cost portfolios, but it doesn't offer a SIPP.

The website is slightly irritating in that you have to login and click through a few pages to see and search their fund selection.

At first glance, a selection of just 550 funds might seem disappointing. However, these are all ETFs, which tend to be lower cost. What's more, it provides enough funds for me to build my low-cost portfolios.

The redeeming factor in terms of website user experience is that you can search funds by ISIN. The fees are competitive as well: another point in its favour.

That lack of a SIPP means that I would need to use a different website for my pension.

A J Bell

Overall Score	**85%**
Fund range	86%
ISA offered	Yes
SIPP offered	Yes
Low platform fees	47%
Ease of use	80%

This has an excellent range of low-cost funds.

The general search facility on the website is the best way to search all funds (ETFs and others) with one ISIN. You don't have to create an account to use it.

Their platform fees appeared to be quite a bit higher than those of other platforms that earned a "yes" from me.

Category: Maybe

I might keep money in these platforms that's already there, but I would put any future investments into a Yes platform.

The Maybe platforms:

Aviva
Barclays
Close Brothers
Fidelity
Halifax
Hargreaves Lansdown
IG
Vanguard

Aviva

Overall Score	**54%**
Fund range	39%
ISA offered	Yes
SIPP offered	Yes
Low platform fees	34%
Ease of use	10%

Reasonable fund selection but a painful user experience.

From what I could see, and I spent A LOT of time trawling through the website, Aviva only includes peer/competitor funds when Aviva itself doesn't provide a similar product.

Aviva's products tended toward the expensive.

If you have the patience and tenacity, you can go through the tedious process of getting to the fund selection and searching for the funds you want.

I could not get the website to return any results for ISINs or full fund names. I had to keep abbreviating the name before sifting through the funds.

At the end of this online torture, I found that Aviva does have a half-decent fund selection. But add in the mediocre pricing that gets less competitive the more you invest, why bother?

Barclays

Overall Score	**62%**
Fund range	54%
ISA offered	Yes
SIPP offered	Yes
Low platform fees	34%
Ease of use	10%

The Barclays website is hard work to use. It claims that there are "c4000 funds" to choose from...if you set up an account then login to see the funds.

The reality I encountered was rather different. Go to this URL, https://www.barclaysinvestments.com/ select your country and investor type and you're presented with a much shorter list. You can search this shorter list by ISIN.

In the case of UK retail investors, it offered fewer than 400 funds. Those 400 funds mostly charged fees that are too high for my liking.

Back in the logged-in version, you have to select Funds and ETFs, etc., and THEN put the ISIN in, and THEN repeat this under the other tabs. Why won't Barclays allow the user to search across all funds for the ISIN?

The Barclays website is not alone in this but that doesn't stop it from being mighty bothersome.

Also, the search results only go up to 20 per page. Loads of refreshing and time wasting. Plus, fund names are abbreviated to make them difficult to comprehend.

And, being Barclays, the website is constantly trying to time you out and log you off if you open any pages in a different tab or window. Very frustrating.

However, you can filter out all funds charging more than, say, 0.50% OCF.

Close Brothers

Overall Score	**52%**
Fund range	23%
ISA offered	Yes
SIPP offered	Yes
Low platform fees	56%
Ease of use	50%

The limited selection of low-cost funds and middling platform fees leave Close Brothers with a Maybe from me.

The website funnels you into providing your personal and bank details before it will tell you what funds you can choose from.

I had to phone up and get the location of their rather good investment search facility https://www.closebrothersam.com/investing-online/investment-search/

Once you've lifted that stone, you can see that Close Brothers has an OK selection of funds. It's almost enough to construct my low-cost Model Portfolios, albeit with blind spots in bonds and alternatives.

Fidelity

Overall Score	**79%**
Fund range	79%
ISA offered	Yes
SIPP offered	Yes
Low platform fees	34%
Ease of use	70%

Fidelity has made massive strides since its decision, 10 years ago, to catch up with competitors on the provision of a platform and low-cost funds for its customers.

My research and analysis suggest that it has overtaken most, never mind caught up. For a large financial institution, that's one heck of an achievement.

The search facility is easy to find and you don't have to login or provide loads of personal details.

However, you DO have to search for the same funds on three different lists (funds, exchange-traded funds (ETFs) and investment trusts).

Also, I encountered a number of problems setting up a SIPP and buying funds with the Fidelity website. I emailed various Fidelity contacts and left voicemail messages over a number of months and heard nothing back, a worrying sign.

The overall website search function at the very top of the home page returns results of funds, at least it does for Fidelity's own funds. But it's not intuitive and I didn't fully test it with every fund ISIN because I have a life.

Halifax

Overall Score	**66%**
Fund range	52%
ISA offered	Yes
SIPP offered	Yes
Low platform fees	13%
Ease of use	100%

Halifax offers a website that is a pleasure to use (others providers please take note). But platform fees are high for portfolios below £50,000, and the website has a blind spot when it comes to global government bonds.

The most important issue here in my opinion is the lack of low-cost global government bond funds in its offering of around 2,700 funds.

Less important is the fixed annual fee of £112. That's roughly three-times the lowest platform fee among the platforms that I reviewed. Once a portfolio exceeds £50,000 though, this becomes a small amount.

Finishing with a huge positive for Halifax: its website. This is how websites should be. It's a pleasure to use. The search box immediately shows the result if it has the fund you enter by ISIN. It has lots of filters on the search facility and you can view 20, 50 or 100 results.

Hargreaves Lansdown

Overall Score	**54%**
Fund range	34%
ISA offered	Yes
SIPP offered	Yes
Low platform fees	21%
Ease of use	50%

High fees and a disappointing range of low-cost funds let Hargreaves Lansdown, er, down.

I expected Hargreaves Lansdown to fare much better what with its high profile. However, I had heard that its fees were confusing and high, but I really didn't expect the fund selection to be as poor as I found it to be, particularly with low-cost UK shares.

There are loads of low-cost funds out there that Hargreaves Lansdown could include but, from what I could find, does not. It has plenty of high-cost ones though.

The website is OK but searching for specific funds could be simpler. You have to go to the overall website search facility rather than mess around with their filters. The website search facility returns results quickly when searching for ISINs.

IG

Overall Score	**55%**
Fund range	35%
ISA offered	Yes
SIPP offered	Yes
Low platform fees	26%
Ease of use	50%

IG was almost a Yes, but its expensive SIPP and administrative glitches when I tried to set up a SIPP earned it a demotion to Maybe.

IG's offering has its roots in share trading, which is reflected in the relatively complex but comprehensive website.

Also, the selection of funds is above average but the fees for ISA and Share Dealing accounts were difficult to fathom; I've gone with my best guess based on their flat custody fee of £24 a quarter (£96 a year).

For SIPPs, the fee is just too high at £175 a year.

If IG had offered a cheaper Global Shares fund, that wouldn't have mattered as much. But the cheapest one it offers has an OCF of 0.10%, double that available with Interactive Investor.

On a positive note, I didn't have to log in to search their ETFs. I did create an account and was able to search for everything using their slightly misleading "Search markets" box. This returned results on all ISINs that I put in.

Vanguard

Overall Score	**49%**
Fund range	12%
ISA offered	Yes
SIPP offered	Yes
Low platform fees	74%
Ease of use	50%

The limited range of funds is not helped by Vanguard apparently hiding some of the ones that I find most attractive.

As the company that invented passive funds in the 1970s, I was expecting Vanguard to do so much better. The late founder, John Bogle, is something of a financial hero for ordinary investors as he accepted lower profits and offered much better value.

Recently, though, the company has ventured into active funds that offer higher profits for them but, well, you know what I think of active funds.

What's more, I'd heard that Vanguard hides or excludes some of its most attractive low-cost funds. Sure enough, I discovered exactly this.

I prefer funds that reinvest the dividends they earn. These "accumulative" or "acc" funds dominate my low-cost portfolios. Several of Vanguard's Acc funds were not shown in search results but you could winkle a few out by searching for ISINs here: https://www.vanguardinvestor.co.uk/search?query=.

What was even more disappointing was that some of the best low-cost funds were impossible for me to find no matter where I looked. If the folk at Vanguard can correct me on this, then great. But the decent folk at *Which?* found the same result.

And that raises the question as to why Vanguard would not make all of its funds available to its own customers on its own platform.

Vanguard offers a range of 70 funds to choose from (not including the 16 ready-made portfolios, which I don't like - see chapter 20). This range includes some of the active (i.e., expensive) funds that Vanguard has started offering lately.

Nevertheless, being Vanguard, there are some attractive low-cost funds available, but not the range available I need to build my low-cost portfolios.

Category: No

I would seriously consider pulling my money out of these platforms and transfering it to one of my "Yes" platforms.

A note on transfering

If I were to transfer from an existing SIPP or ISA, I would follow the instructions on my new account of how to transfer existing SIPP or ISA investments to my new provider. I would be unlikely to sell the investments and then transfer the cash. Doing that could destroy my tax advantages or incur lots of fees.
Before you do anything like this, get professional advice.

A few of these "No" platforms offer relatively substantial payments to anyone who recommends them. But they don't offer a good enough selection of low-cost funds for me to set up the low-cost portfolios that I've talked about in this book. Hence, I cannot recommend them.

The No platforms:

BestInvest
Charles Stanley
HSBC Direct Invest
Santander
Trading212

BestInvest

Overall Score	**43%**
Fund range	6%
ISA offered	Yes
SIPP offered	Yes
Low platform fees	30%
Ease of use	50%

Easy to use but insufficient fund choice.

The BestInvest website is very user-friendly. You can download a PDF of all funds the company offers.

However, almost all the funds are expensive and, therefore, don't make the cut for my low-cost portfolios.

Charles Stanley

Overall Score	**42%**
Fund range	6%
ISA offered	Yes
SIPP offered	Yes
Low platform fees	39%
Ease of use	50%

Very disappointing offering.

The online experience is tiresome, although it's not as bad as some. What really lets Charles Stanley down for me is the miserly offering of just 22 low-cost passive or ETF funds in their "preferred list" of just 76.

If the company offers more than this, I'd be really keen to hear how to find them as that would make a heck of a difference to my opinion of the company's offering. Those funds that I could find were predictably expensive.

On the upside, you can view some of the funds without logging in. Back on the downside, I had to search by their restricted topics, I couldn't search by specific funds.

The ISIN sometimes appears at the top of the fund that you've clicked on but not often enough. Usually, I'd have to dig around in various financial documents, such as the Factsheet or Key Investor Information Document (see Glossary), to find the ISIN.

HSBC InvestDirect

Overall Score	**45%**
Fund range	10%
ISA offered	Yes
SIPP offered	Yes
Low platform fees	56%
Ease of use	40%

The impression I got from HSBC's offering was that it doesn't want retail investors' money.

The range of 500 funds appeared to me to be a limited selection of expensive funds.

If my experience is anything to go by, HSBC's biggest howler is that it appears to exclude many of its cheapest funds, and those of its investment partner, on its own platform for its own customers.

In other words, from what I could tell, HSBC's customers can only buy expensive funds.

Remember, most of the investments I'm looking at charge an OCF of no more than 0.10%. If someone at HSBC can correct me on my assessment of its website, I'd love to hear from them and put this right.

One last negative; the list of funds doesn't include ISINs and there's no search facility that I could find. You have to look at every fund to find the ones you want.

Plenty of room for improvement.

Santander

Overall Score	**29%**
Fund range	15%
ISA offered	Yes
SIPP offered	No
Low platform fees	39%
Ease of use	20%

Santander more or less failed across the board of my needs.

It offers a limited range of expensive funds, requires the user to set up an account to see what funds are on offer, and does not offer a SIPP.

It offers "Over 1,000 funds" of which around 820 charge more than the maximum 0.20% OCF I look for on most of the funds included in my low-cost portfolios.

The platform fees are average.

Trading212

Overall Score	**34%**
Fund range	26%
ISA offered	Yes
SIPP offered	No
Low platform fees	0%
Ease of use	80%

Too few funds and the highest fees of the platforms I reviewed.

The stock selection is too limited for me to be able to build my low-cost portfolios.

I also found it to be the most expensive platform for portfolios up to £50,000.

The website is very easy to use, however, with an effective search facility that returns results almost before you've finished typing them.

Category: Did Not Qualify (DNQ)

These companies do a lot of marketing so there's a fair chance you'll have heard of them. I've included these so you don't wonder why I haven't mentioned them.

They include some that would pay me a really good fee to send you in their direction. But they don't qualify for my low-cost portfolios because they only offer ready-made funds.

As I have mentioned earlier, I don't like ready-made funds because they don't allow me to copy the average view of asset allocation among banks and investment companies.

Also, I'm not convinced that they charge low enough fees.

The platforms that did not qualify for my low-cost portfolios were:

Moneybox
Moneyfarm
Nutmeg
Wealthify

Bottom line

Be careful as to the platforms you choose. There are some alluring but expensive (and sometimes downright awful) platforms out there.

PART NINE

Setting Up Investments

32. Step-by-step set-up process
33. Next steps

32 Step-by-step set-up process

In this part, I'll go through the steps required to open an account, upload money and set up the portfolio on one of the platforms that did well in my review, namely **Interactive Investor.**

The process

I will:

- Set up my account
- Identify the most appropriate Model Portfolio to copy
- Identify the funds I want to buy
- Work out how much of each fund I want to buy
- Buy the funds
- Spend 12 months living my life, ignoring my investments.

I share real portfolios on the website

I've set up portfolios using my own money on each of these platforms to see how they compare. I share the results on my website (address at the bottom of every other page).

The website is free to use. I am not sponsored or employed by any of the companies with whom I have invested my own money.

The following is just one example from my Yes platforms. I consider all my Yes platforms to be similarly decent.

Setting up an account

I go to the Interactive Investor website here {affiliate link*}

**Links to the internet that have an asterisk (*) denote an affiliate link. This helps to keep the website free to use as the links are tracked to that website. Using the affiliate link can (but not always) lead to a payment to the investwithoutbeingrippedoff.com website.*

IMPORTANT: the assessments made on investments and platforms are based on how good they are on what they pay. This is borne out by the fact that:

- The highest-paying affiliate links belong to platforms that did not score highly enough in my review to include them in my list of Yes platforms in Part 8 of this book, and

- I have been entirely transparent about how I assessed the platforms, so you can verify my findings and drop me a line via the website if you think I've missed something or if something needs to be updated.

Cash allocation note

In the following, I set up a SIPP account. This incurs higher costs than some other investment accounts.

After monitoring the costs for a couple of months, it became clear that I needed to allocate nearer £200 rather than £100 to my cash allocation to cover costs for 12 months.

In the following step-by-step example, I only leave £100 in the account when I set this up. If I were to do this again, I would knock £100 off my allocation to alternatives and add that to my allocation to cash.

I click on the "Services" tab at the top of the page and then click the appropriate one of the following options:

- Stocks and Shares ISA
- Trading Account (i.e., a general investment account)
- SIPP

In the following example, I've chosen to set up a SIPP.

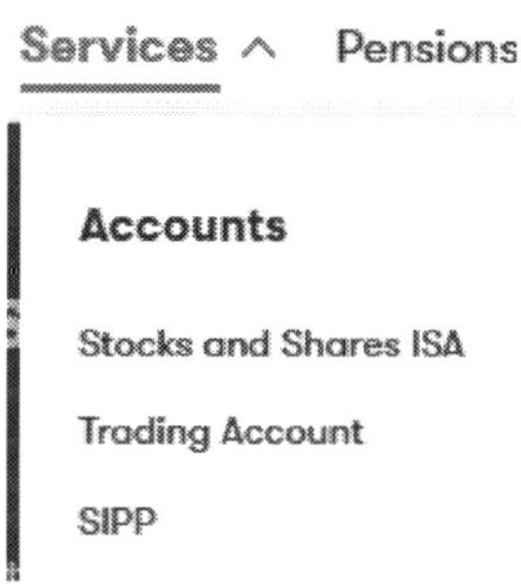

I then go through the process of submitting my personal, tax, employment, National Insurance and debit card details.

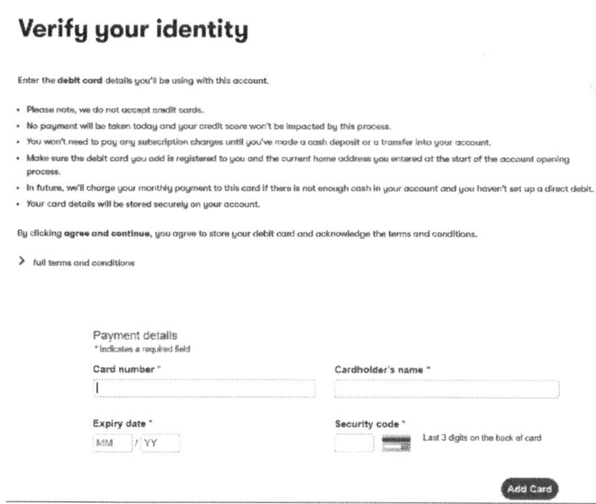

Once I've uploaded these details, confirmed my identity (by submitting my driving licence or passport information) and uploaded some money, I'm ready to allocate the money to the appropriate funds.

Using the most appropriate model portfolio

In this example, I'm going to invest £10,000. Having completed the risk questionnaire earlier in this book, I have confirmed that my risk tolerance is "higher".

Therefore, the model portfolio I'm going to copy is the Tier 2, Higher-Risk Model Portfolio (from chapter 26 in this book):

Tier 2: Between £5,000 and £15,000 to invest

Risk level	Cash	Global Gov. Bonds	Global Corp. Bonds	Global Shares	Alternatives
Lower	1%	41%	25%	33%	0%
Medium	1%	21%	22%	51%	5%
Higher	1%	8%	8%	78%	5%

Identifying the funds I need to buy

Looking at the lists of funds in Chapter 23, I can see that these are the cheapest funds that I need to buy for my new portfolio:

Asset Class	Fund	OCF	ISIN
Global Government Bonds	Amundi Index Solutions - Amundi Prime Global Govies UCITS ETF DR (PRIG)	0.08%	LU1931975236
Global Corporate Bonds	L&G ESG GBP Corporate Bond UCITS ETF	0.08%	GB00BPFJD529
Global shares	Amundi Index Solutions - Amundi Prime Global UCITS ETF DR (PRIW)	0.78%	LU1931974692
Alternatives	iShares Developed Real Estate Index Fund (IE) Class D GBP	0.05%	GB00B5BFJG71

Work out how much of each fund I need to buy

Trust me, this is a simple calculation.

The simple calculation

If you wanted to know what 1% of a number is, you'd multiply the number by 0.01. For example, 1% of £9,337 is 0.01 x £9,337 which equals £93.37.

Here are some more examples:

2% of £9,337 is 0.02 x £9,337 which equals £186.74
87% of £9,337 is 0.88 x £9,337 which equals £8,211.28
100% of £9,337 is 1.00 x £9,337 which equals £9,337

The calculation in my new £10,000 portfolio

I want:

- £100-£200 in cash, assume £100 in this instance to keep the maths simple for this demo. If it were a SIPP, I would allocate nearer £200 and reduce alternatives by £100.
- 8% in global government bonds i.e., 0.08 x £10,000 = £800
- 8% in global corporate bonds i.e., 0.08 x £10,000 = £800
- 78% in global shares i.e., 0.78 x £10,000 = £7,800
- 5% in alternatives i.e., 0.05 x £10,000 = £500

To make sure I've got the calculations correct, I add the numbers up. They should add up to £10,000 (including the cash allocaiton).

To show you what this means, here's the fund table again, but with the allocations added:

Asset Class	Fund	OCF	ISIN	£ Allocation
Cash	Leave this as cash in the account. Don't buy anything with it.			£100-£200
Global Gov. Bonds	Amundi Index Solutions - Amundi Prime Global Govies UCITS ETF DR (PRIG)	0.08%	LU1931975236	£800
Global Corp. Bonds	L&G ESG GBP Corporate Bond UCITS ETF	0.08%	IE00BLRPQM83	£800
Global shares	Amundi Index Solutions - Amundi Prime Global UCITS ETF DR (PRIW)	0.78%	LU1931974692	£7,800
Alternatives	iShares Developed Real Estate Index Fund (IE) Class D GBP	0.05%	GB00B5BFJG71	£500

The allocations won't match precisely

I'll aim to buy as close to £800 of global government bonds, £800 of global corporate bonds, £7,800 of global shares and £500 of alternatives as I can.

But in each instance, the actual amount I buy will be slightly less. This will leave me with slightly more than £100 in cash in the account. I add some money to this to bring it up to around £170 because it's a SIPP account and I want to be sure I've covered the costs for the coming 12 months.

I happen to have more than £10,000 in my Interactive Investor SIPP screenshots shown below because I was playing around to see how things worked. Ignore that!

As part of testing the Interactive Investor platform, I set up and put some money into a SIPP account. I then transferred a further £10,000 from my existing SIPP on a different platform.

Anyhoo, let's assume we're logged in and get on with the process.

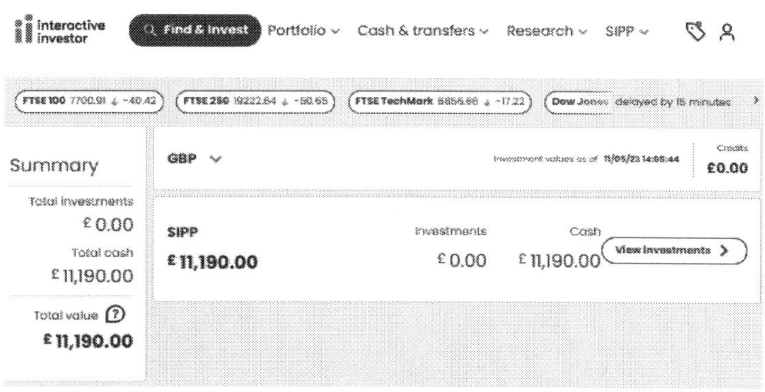

I click "Find & Invest"

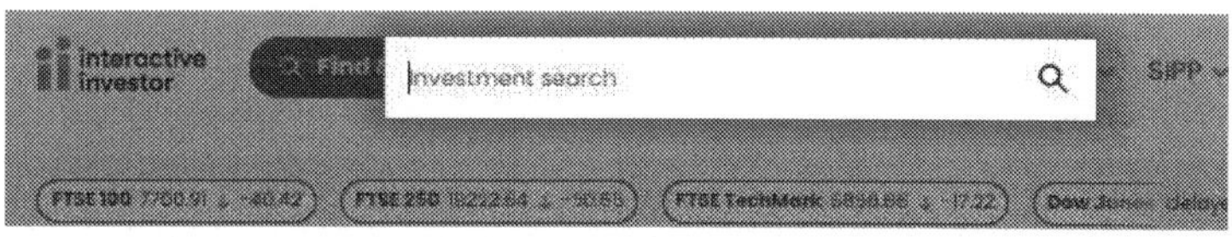

Next, I enter the first ISIN and the fund automatically appears below:

I buy and sell funds between 10am and 2pm

The market for shares, bonds and funds opens at 8am, UK time. For the first hour or so, prices of everything can jump around as big traders (banks and the like) digest news that's come out since the market closed the previous day.

I prefer to wait until that's all calmed down and prices have settled into what buyers and sellers generally agree to be a fair price for the time being.

The next jumble of chaos comes when the US markets open at 9:30am New York time which equates to 2:30pm UK time.

Rip-Off Tip-Off

I prefer to buy between 10am and 2pm UK time because things tend to have settled down by then and I like to keep things simple.

And, in case you hadn't guessed, markets are closed on public holidays and weekends. Some funds can be bought outside trading hours and orders can be placed to buy them when markets open the next day, but I just buy when the market is open and relatively quiet.

Now I click on that fund, which brings me to the "Place an Order" option

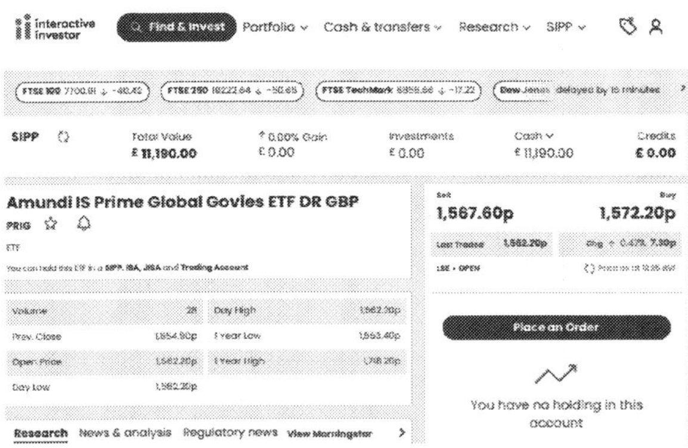

I then click the blue "Place an Order" button and the following screen appears:

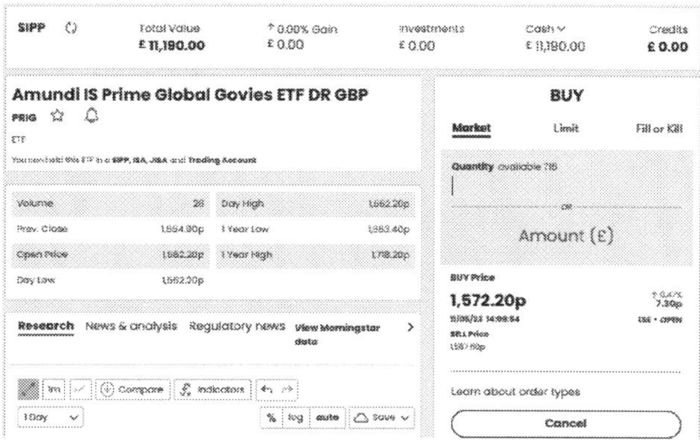

At this stage, I type in the amount.

I place an order for £800 as this aligns with the table a few pages earlier that is appropriate for me - a higher-risk investor with £10,000 to invest.

I type "800" into the "Amount (£)" line. The website automatically tells me roughly how many units of the fund I can buy for that, in this instance, it estimates 51 units (the price of units changes all the time, so £800 might buy more or fewer units the next day):

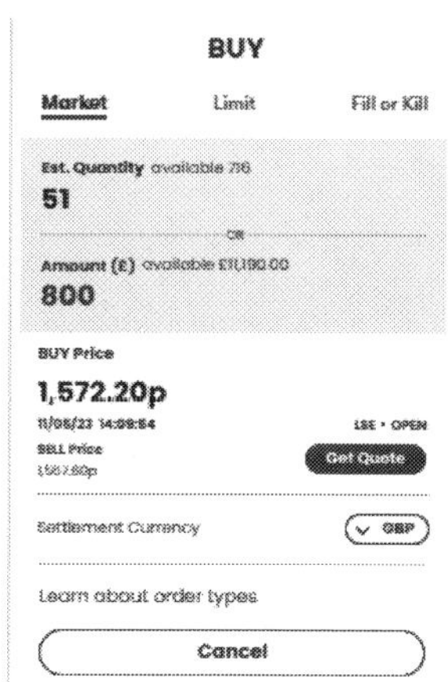

I then make sure that the "Market" tab is selected at the top of the screen, i.e. I check the word is in a bold font and underlined in blue.

This means that the price quote I get will be whatever the latest price is in the market. I'm not interested in "Limit" or "Fill or Kill".

These are means by which I could try to get a better price, but it's too time-consuming and complicated for the sake of a small, short-term advantage which is not guaranteed anyway.

Next, I click the blue "Get Quote" button which brings this up on screen:

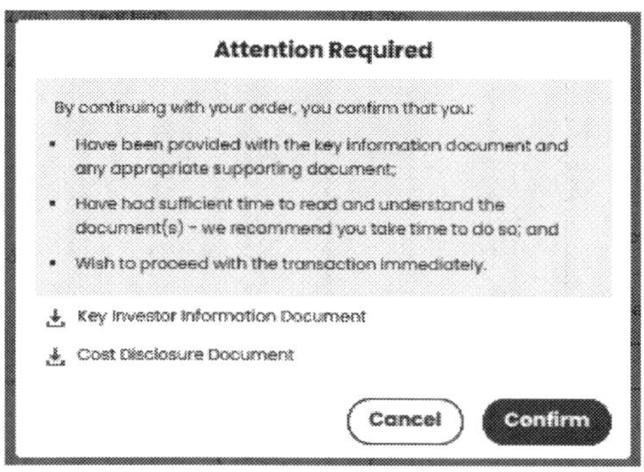

I can download and read the documents and would if I weren't familiar with them and what they cover.

Once I'm happy with the documents, I click the blue "Confirm" button, which brings up this screen:

I have 15 seconds in which to click the blue "Place Order" button.

I won't allow myself to be pressured by this.

If I'm unsure about anything or want to double-check that I'm buying the correct amount of the correct fund, I can just let the clock run down which would bring up this screen:

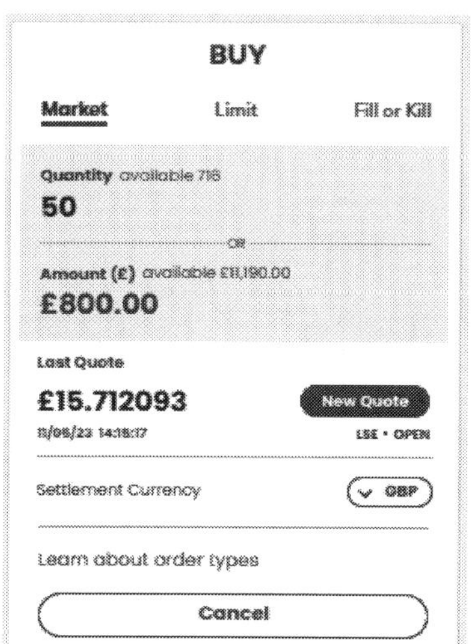

I can then click "New Quote" which will bring up the 15-second "Place Order" box again.

Once I click the blue "Place Order" button, I get this screen:

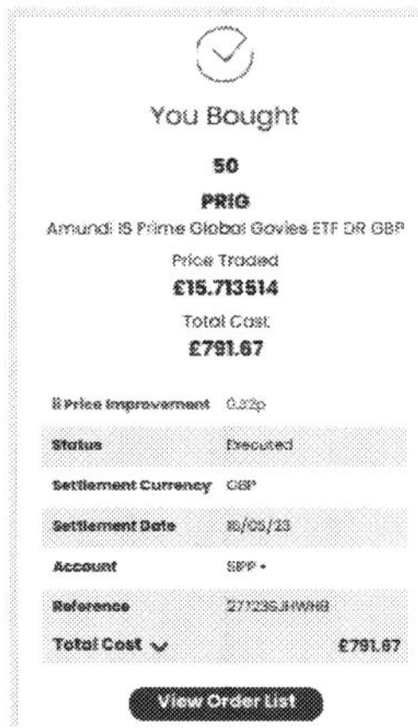

In the end, I only got 50 units of the fund, not the 51 that the website originally estimated. I'm not worried about that difference. The total cost was £791.67. I have to click the blue arrow next to the words "Total Cost" to see how the cost breaks down:

Interactive Investor charged £6 for the transaction.

If I click the blue "View Order List" I can see the one fund that I've bought:

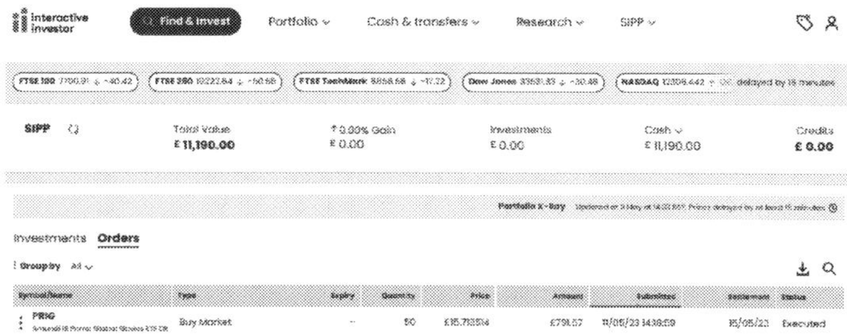

Now I can repeat the process for the next fund I want to buy: £800-worth of the global corporate bond fund with the ISIN IE00BLRPQM83.

I click on the blue "Find & Invest" button at the top of the screen and enter the ISIN IE00BLRPQM83:

I then click on the fund that comes up:

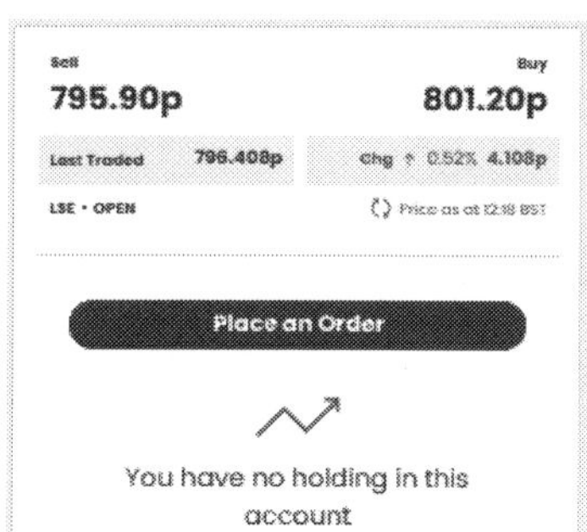

It's still saying "You have no holding in this account". This message means that I have no holding of *this specific fund* in my account, which is correct.

I click the blue "Place an Order" and insert the £800 in the "Amount (£)" box:

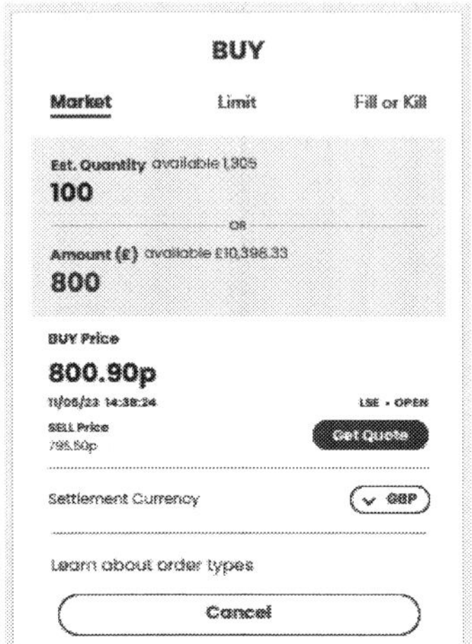

Next, I click "Get Quote" which brings up the "Attention Required" box again:

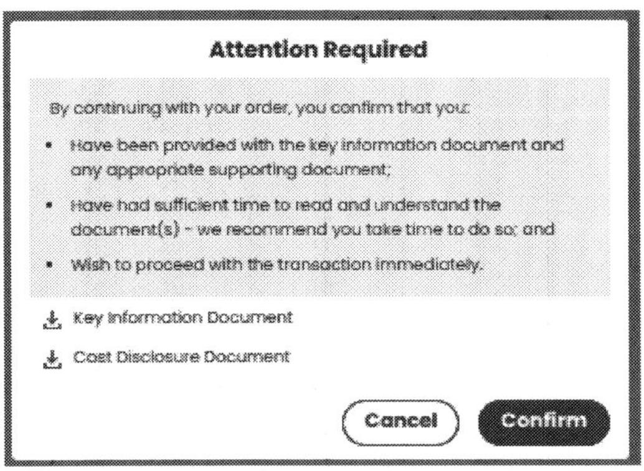

I'm now happy to click the blue "Confirm" button which brings up the 15-seconds "Place Order" screen:

I click the blue "Place Order" button which brings up the "You Bought" box:

Next up, I enter £7,800 in the global shares fund with the ISIN LU1931974692.

I then click the blue "Place an Order" button:

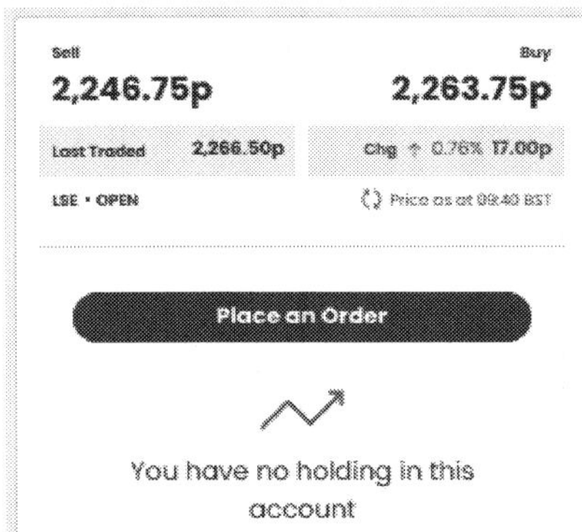

I type £7,800 into the "Amount (£)" box:

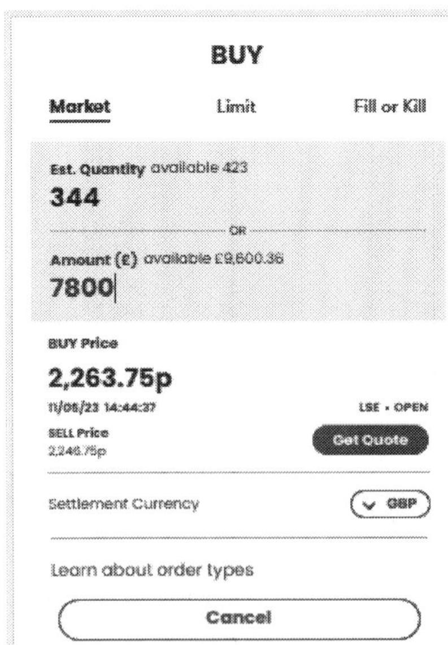

Now I click "Get Quote" which brings up the "Attention Required" box:

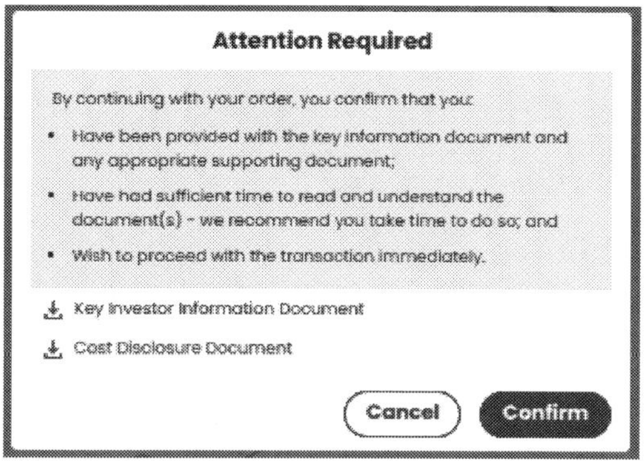

I click "Confirm", which then brings up the 15 seconds "Place Order" box:

I now click "Place Order", which brings up the "You Bought" box:

The fourth and final fund I want to buy is the alternatives i.e., real estate, fund with the ISIN GB00B5BFJG71.

You know the tune by now, so sing along.

Click the blue "Find & Invest" button at the top of the screen and enter the ISIN:

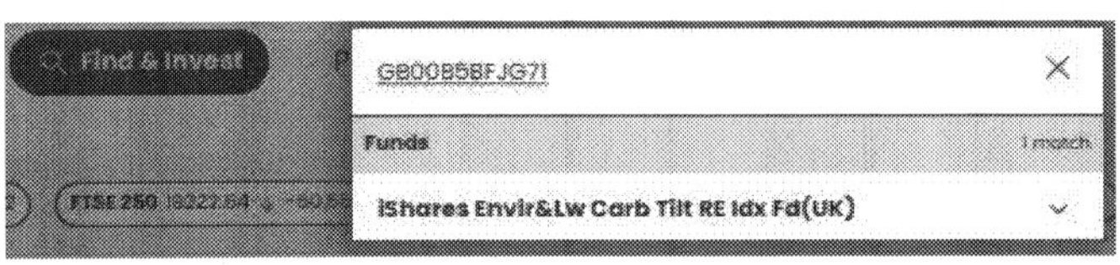

This fund is priced once a day. The other funds I've bought are traded all the time, so their prices go up and down throughout the day.

Hence the process of buying this fund is slightly different.

The first small difference is that I have to click the fund name which reveals the actual fund in a drop-down list (albeit a list of one fund):

Now I can click on the blue fund name. This prompts the "Place an Order" box to appear:

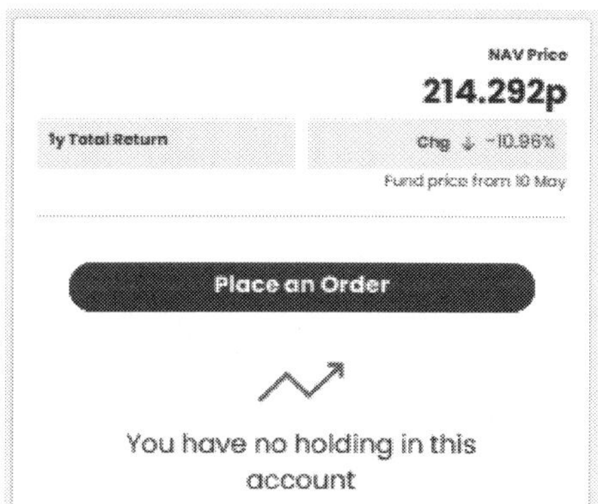

I click "Place an Order", and then type £500 into the "Amount (£)" box:

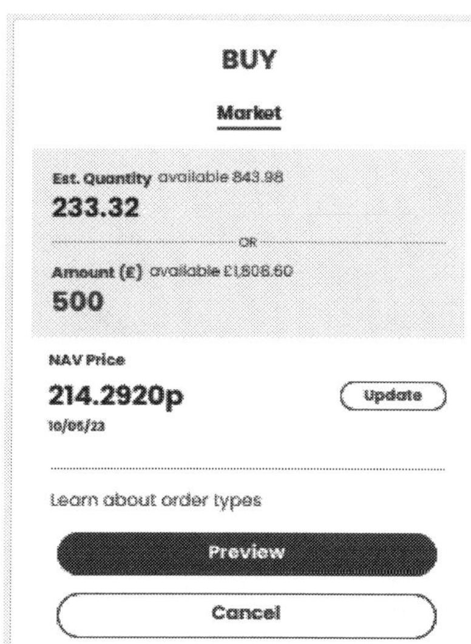

The second slight difference with this fund is that I have to click the "Preview" button. This brings up the first of two "Attention Required" screens:

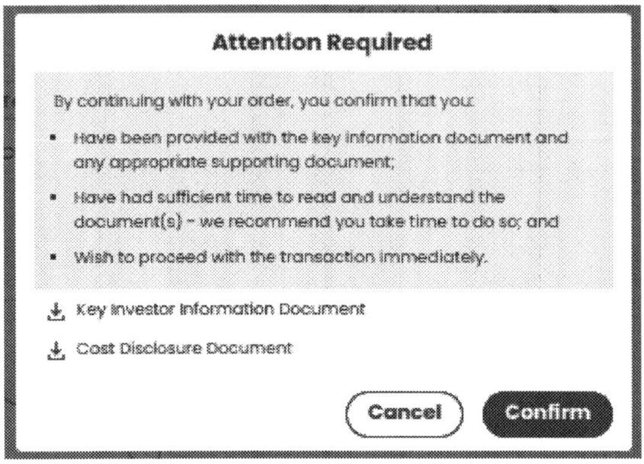

I now click the blue "Confirm" button to bring up this screen:

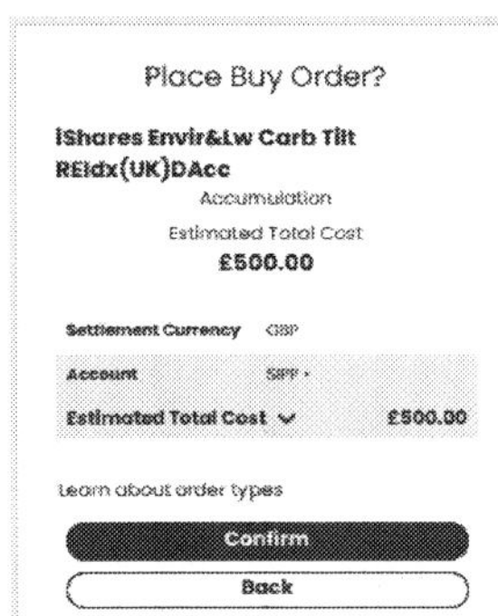

You should note that there is no estimate of how many units the £500 will buy because the fund hasn't been priced for the day.

This isn't anything to worry about, it's just a different pricing process. You put your money in the box and wait to see how much it buys over the coming 24 hours or so.

I then click the "Confirm" button which brings up a different "Attention Required" message:

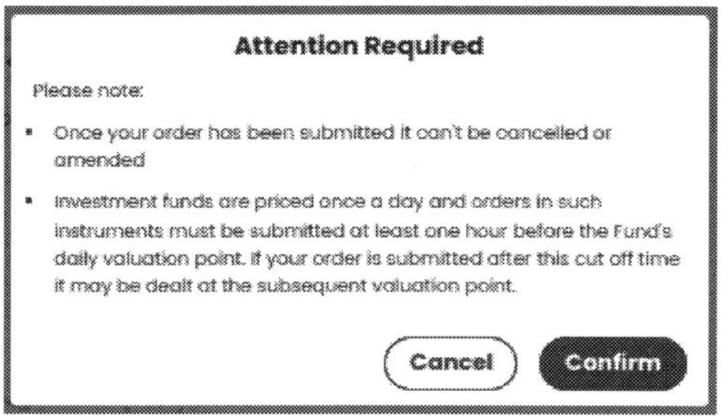

The final screen is a "You've placed an order to Buy" screen:

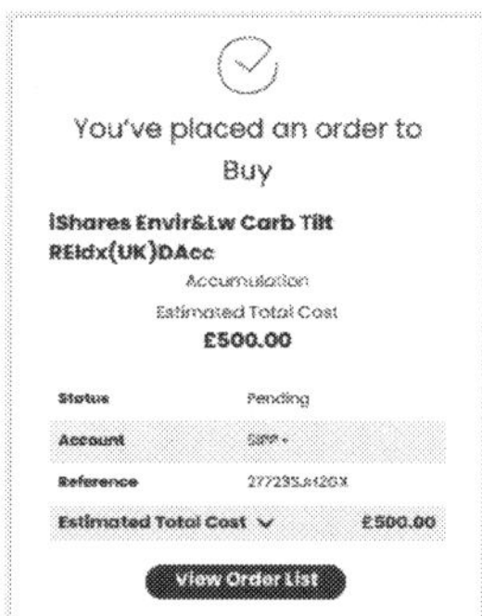

Now I have placed all four orders, it's time to take a look at the order list again:

There are only three orders placed

That's coz I'm waiting for a day or so until the real estate fund is priced and my order is completed. I'll come back a couple of days later and have a look to make sure it's gone through.

To see what orders I have placed but that have not yet completed, I click the "Portfolio" tab at the top of the screen and then click "Orders":

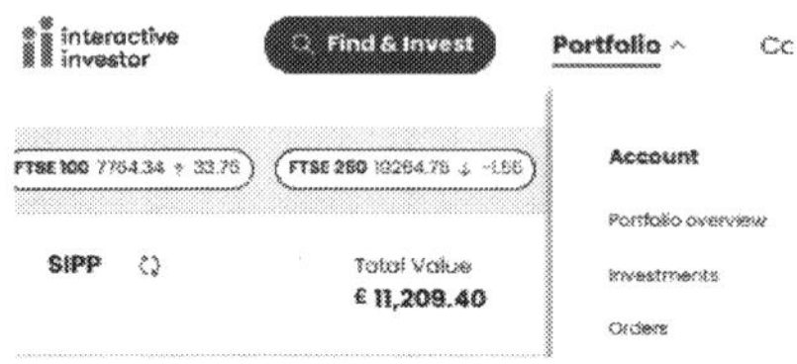

This shows me that I do indeed have one order pending that has not yet completed.

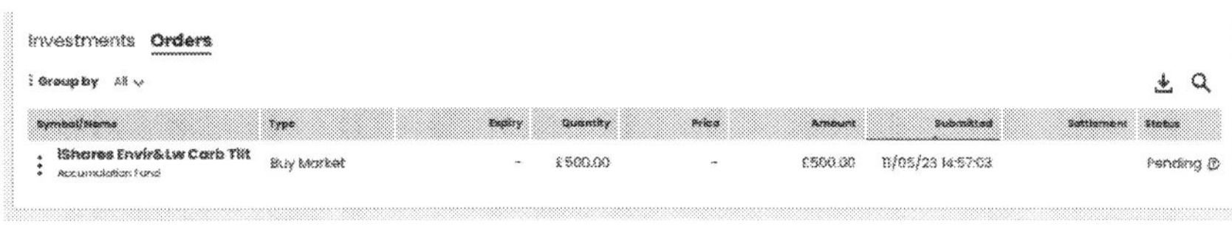

I have made a 0.69% or £64.66 loss

This is because the investment company makes money from you whenever you buy or sell something. There are two main ways in which it does this:

- Buy/sell spread. If you want to buy a fund that has a "mid-price" of, say, £10, that's not what you can actually buy or sell it for.
    - ◊ The company will sell it to you at its "buy-price" of, say, £10.50.
    - ◊ And it will buy it from you at its "sell-price" of, say, £9.50.

- Transaction fee. This varies from platform to platform. As I've shown above, the transaction fee with Interactive Investor is £6.

I don't worry about this small loss because I'm only going to buy funds when I have at least £500 to invest (preferably more).

If I have less than £500, I'll wait until I have at least £500 to invest before buying anything, otherwise I'll be losing too big a portion of that money in the buy/sell spreads and transaction fees.

A couple of days later

As a property fund that's priced on a daily basis, this order took a couple of days to go through. Once that went through, my orders list looked like this:

Investments Orders — Portfolio X-Ray >

Group by All

Updated at 16 May at 09:42 BST. Prices delayed by at least 15 minutes

Symbol/Name	Quantity	Price	Day Price Change	% Day Price Change	Book Cost	Market Value	Gain/Loss	% Gain/Loss
GBPC L&G ESG GBP Corporate Bond ETF	99	793.10p	-2.50p ↓	-0.31 ↓	£797.97	£785.17	£-12.80	-1.60 ↓
iShares Envir&Lw Carb Tilt Accumulation Fund	230.209	214.957p	0.37p ↑	0.17 ↑	£500.00	£494.85	£-5.15	-1.03 ↓
PRIG Amundi IS Prime Global Govies ETF DR	50	1,556.20p	-11.40p ↓	-0.73 ↓	£791.67	£778.10	£-13.57	-1.71 ↓
PRIW Amundi IS Prime Global ETF DR GBP	345	2,266.25p	8.13p ↑	0.36 ↑	£7,791.76	£7,818.56	£26.80	0.34 ↑

There are some minor losses and gains shown in the "Gains/Losses" right-hand column. I really don't give a tinker's cuss about them. I'm set up for the next 12 months, so I can get on with my life and forget about my investments in the meantime.

Performance and cost updates on my website

I update the performance and costs of this investment on the website so that you can see how it's doing and what it costs.

Bottom line

At first glance, this might seem confusing or daunting. It's not if you follow along. If you think I haven't explained it properly, go to my website (listed at the foot of this page) and drop me a line.

33

Next steps

Adding more money before I rebalance

I'd use my common sense here. Bearing in mind that I pay around £8 every time I buy (or sell) something, I wouldn't buy more funds unless I had at least £500 to invest in one go.

Let's look at it continuing from the set-up process that I went through in the previous chapter.

An additional £500 to invest

If I had another £500, I'd probably buy just global shares. Then, when I had another £500, I'd buy £250 of global government bonds and £250 of global corporate bonds.

An additional £1,000 to invest

If I had another, say, £1,000, I'd buy £780-worth of global shares and split the rest between global government bonds and global corporate bonds (i.e., £110 on each).

The property allocation is only 5%. That would equate to £50 from my additional £1,000. I'm not going to lose £8 of that £50 on transaction costs. I'd probably wait until my annual rebalancing to adjust the allocation to property.

With smaller sums like this, my priority would be to keep investing, and not worry too much about the exact allocations.

An additional £5,000 or more to invest

Once the amount that I have in additional funds to invest exceeds £5,000, I'd allocate in line with my model portfolio.

In the examples I've shown, that's:

- 78% to global shares i.e., £3,900
- 8% to global government bonds i.e., £400
- 8% to global corporate bonds i.e., £400
- 5% to property i.e., £250.

Annual rebalancing

I addressed this in Chapter 29. It's a way of making sure that I'm keeping my allocation in line with my risk preferences.

It also allows me to adjust my long-term allocation to match what the big investment and banking houses are doing (but without paying them loads of money).

Bottom line

Keep investing money every time you have enough to justify the transaction fees.

PART TEN

Conclusion

34. Living your life

34 Living your life

I hope that what I've written will help provide insight from an industry insider on how to keep more of your money, while also not having to spend time worrying or even thinking about your investments.

As I've said before in this book, I don't want to spend more time than I absolutely have to thinking about my investments, finance, etc.

The way I set up my investments is based on my desire to forget about them. That's why it's so important that I lay the foundations (clear bad debt, set up the cash buffer) and find a portfolio that has the right level of risk for me.

If there's one thought I would leave you with, it would be this:

***start* NOW.**

Whatever stage you're at, be it assessing your circumstances, setting up a cash buffer or starting to put money aside, I urge you to get on with it.

The precise actions in this book might not be for you, but they should help you to understand how things can work without all the jargon, webinars, newsletters and fluff that most banks and investment companies are so keen on churning out.

Finally, if you're ever in doubt about any of this, get professional independent advice. Be careful about agreeing to a percentage of your investments. I'd much rather spend, say, £1,000-£1,500 on upfront advice and then only consider getting more advice if I felt really needed it in a year or two's time.

Good luck! And remember, you can get updates on the funds and portfolios I like, as well as the progress, performance and costs of the example fund I covered in Part Nine of this book, at the website (address at the foot of every other page) that accompanies this book.

Ciao.

PART ELEVEN

Appendix

Appendix 1. I save 90% on fees
Appendix 2. The low-cost funds I like
Appendix 3. Useful resources

A1 I save 90% in fees

Active funds average Ongoing Charges Figure (OCF):0.89% (or 89 basis points, one basis point = 0.01%)
Passive funds average OCF: 0.15% (or 15 basis points)

My portfolios weighted OCF: 0.05% to 0.08% (or 5 to 8 basis points)

By paying no more than 8 basis points, I make a 90% saving on the Ongoing Charges Figure.

My calculations

The weighted OCF on the funds I buy range of between 0.08% for a small, lower-risk portfolio (the highest OCF in my portfolios at the time of writing) and 0.05% for a £50,000+, higher-risk portfolio.

Active funds, according to the FCA's own study, charged an average OCF of 0.89%. I'm not convinced that that average applies to what ordinarly investors, like you and me, pay. For us, I think it's more like between 1.2% and 2.2%.

Tier 1: Between £1,000 and £5,000 to invest

Risk level	Cash	Mixed Bonds	Global Shares	**Weighted OCF**
Lower	4%	64%	32%	**0.08%**
Medium	4%	43%	53%	**0.07%**
Higher	4%	18%	78%	**0.06%**
OCF	0%	0.10%	0.05%	

The calculation methodology

Weighted OCFs = {asset class allocation1 x OCF1} + {asset class allocation2 x OCF2}

Lower- risk allocation weighted OCF
= (64% x 0.10%) + (32% x 0.05%)
= 0.064% + 0.016%
= 0.080%

Medium-risk allocation weighted OCF
= (43% x 0.10%) + (53% x 0.05%)
= 0.043% + 0.027%
= 0.070%

Higher-risk allocation weighted OCF
= (18% x 0.10%) + (78% x 0.05%)
= 0.018% + 0.039% = 0.057%

Tier 2: Between £5,000 and £15,000 to invest

Risk level	Cash	Global Gov. Bonds	Global Corp. Bonds	Global Shares	Alternatives	**Weighted OCF**
Lower	2%	40%	25%	33%	0%	**0.06%**
Medium	2%	21%	22%	50%	5%	**0.07%**
Higher	2%	7%*	8%	78%	5%	**0.06%**
OCF	0%	0.05%	0.11%	0.05%	0.24%	

**This differs from the 8% that I allocated in my two examples in Part Nine of this book because the example here allows for 2%, not 1%, to be allocated to cash.*

Tier 3: Between £15,000 and £50,000 to invest

	Cash	Short-term Bonds	Global Gov. Bonds	Global Corp. Bonds	Global Shares	Alternatives	Weighted OCF
Lower	1%	18%	24%	24%	26%	7%	0.08%
Medium	1%	5%	17%	22%	50%	5%	0.07%
Higher	1%	2%	6%	6%	80%	5%	0.06%
OCF	0%	0.06%	0.05%	0.11%	0.05%	0.24%	

Tier 4: From £50,000 upwards

	Cash	Short-term Bonds	UK Sov Bonds	Global Sov Bonds	UK Corp bonds	Global Corp Bonds	UK Shares	Global Shares	Alts	**Weighted OCF**
Low	1%	17%	10%	14%	11%	14%	9%	17%	7%	**0.06%**
Med	1%	5%	7%	10%	9%	12%	17%	34%	5%	**0.06%**
Hig	1%	2%	2%	4%	2%	4%	23%	57%	5%	**0.05%**
OCF	0%	0.06%	0.05%	0.05%	0.08%	0.11%	0.05%	0.05%	0.24%	

A2 The low-cost funds I like

The "average" annual Ongoing Charges Figure (OCF) for an active fund is 0.89%. The low-cost funds I like start at 0.05%. Don't be ripped off. For updates on these funds, get my free monthly (mercifully short) newsletter-me-bob at the website.

Short-term bonds funds

Fund	OCF	ISIN
L&G UK Gilt 0-5 Year UCITS EFT	0.06%	IE00BLRPQK69
Invesco UK Gilt 1-5 Year UCITS ETF GBP Inc (GLT5)	0.06%	IE00BG0TQ445
Invesco US Treasury Bond 1-3 Year UCITS ETF USD Dist (TR3G)	0.06%	IE00BF2FNG46
iShares $ Treasury Bond 1-3yr UCITS ETF USD (Acc) B	0.07%	IE00B3VWN179
Lyxor UK Government Bond 0-5Y (DR) UCITS ETF - Dist-GBP (GIL5)	0.07%	LU1439943090
iShares UK Gilts 0-5yr UCITS ETF	0.09%	IE00BMVJSD83
"iShares £ Ultrashort Bond UCITS ETF GBP (Dist)"	0.09%	IE00BCRY6441
USD Corporate 1-3 Year Bond UCITS ETF USD Accuimulation (VSCA)	0.09%	IE00BGYWSV06
abrdn Short Dated Sterling Corporate Bond Tracker Fund B Acc	0.10%	GB00BGMK1956
Sterling Short-Term Money Market Fund	0.12%	GB00BGB6GZ57
UK S/T Invm Grd Bd Indx £ Acc	0.12%	IE00B9M1BB17
L&G Short Dated £ Corporate Bd Idx I Acc	0.14%	GB00BKGR3H21
abrdn Sterling Money Market Fund	0.15%	GB00B1C42332
ICS £ Ultra Shrt Bd Sel Acc	0.15%	IE00B05LZH92
Short Term Fixed Inc Y Acc	0.15%	GB00BMN51H58
SPDR® Bloomberg 1-5 Year Gilt UCITS ETF (GLTS)	0.15%	IE00B6YX5K17
Global Short-Term Bond Index Fund	0.15%	IE00BH65QG55

UK government bonds funds

Fund	OCF	ISIN
Lyxor Core UK Government Bond (DR) UCITS ETF - Dist-GBP (GILS)	0.05%	LU1407892592
Invesco UK Gilts UCITS ETF GBP Acc (GLTA)	0.06%	IE00BG0TQD32
iShares Core UK Gilts UCITS ETF	0.07%	IE00B1FZSB30
U.K. Gilt UCITS ETF (VGOV)	0.07%	IE00B42WWV65
LEGAL & GENERAL ALL STOCKS GILT INDEX TRUST CLASS C - ACCUMULATION (GBP)	0.08%	GB00BG0QNW27

Fidelity Index UK Gilt Fund P GBP Acc	0.10%	GB00BMQ57G79
iShares UK Gilts All Stks Idx (UK) D Acc	0.11%	GB00B83HGR24
SPDR® Bloomberg UK Gilt UCITS ETF (GLTY)	0.15%	IE00B3W74078
U.K. Government Bond Index Fund	0.12%	IE00B1S75374
UK Gilt Index Fund	0.13%	GB00B80QG383
Fidelity UK Gilt W Acc	0.15%	GB0033144410
L&G All Stocks Gilt Index I Acc	0.15%	GB00B8344798
SPDR® Bloomberg UK Gilt UCITS ETF (GLTY)	0.15%	IE00B3W74078

Global government bonds funds

Fund	OCF	ISIN
Amundi Index Solutions - Amundi Prime Global Govies UCITS ETF DR (PRIG)	0.05%	LU1931975236
ISHARES OVERSEAS GOVERNMENT BOND INDEX CLASS H - ACCUMULATION (GBP)	0.11%	GB00BPFJD859
iShares Overseas Govt Bd Indx (UK) D Acc	0.11%	GB00B849C803
abrdn Global Government Bond Tracker Fund B GBP Acc	0.14%	GB00BK80KQ76
UBS (Lux) Fund Solutions - J.P. Morgan Global Government ESG Liquid Bond UCITS ETF, class (USD) A-acc	0.15%	LU1974693662
iShares Global Govt Bond UCITS ETF	0.20%	IE00BYZ28V50
iShares Global Govt Bond UCITS ETF	0.20%	IE00B3F81K65

Mixed bonds funds

Fund	OCF	ISIN
L&G ESG GBP Corporate Bond UCITS ETF	0.09%	IE00BLRPQM83
iShares Core Global Aggregate Bond UCITS ETF GBP Hedged (Dist) (AGBP)	0.10%	IE00BF540Y54
Global Aggregate Bond UCITS ETF (VAGS)	0.10%	IE00BG47K971
SPDR® Bloomberg Global Aggregate Bond UCITS ETF USD unhedged (GLBL)	0.10%	IE00B43QJJ40
U.K. Investment Grade Bond Index Fund	0.12%	IE00B1S74Q32
Euro Investment Grade Bond Index Fund - Accumulation	0.12%	IE00BFRTD839
Global Bond Index Fund	0.15%	IE00B50W2R13
Global Aggregate Bond Index Fund	0.20%	IE00BF5DZ143

UK corporate bonds funds

Fund	OCF	ISIN
LEGAL & GENERAL STERLING CORPORATE BOND INDEX	0.08%	GB00BG0QPD77
L&G ESG GBP Corporate Bond UCITS ETF	0.09%	IE00BLRPQM83
Invesco GBP Corporate Bond UCITS ETF Dist (IGCB)	0.10%	IE00BKW9SW28

Invesco GBP Corporate Bond ESG UCITS ETF Dist (IGBE)	0.10%	IE00BKW9SV11
ISHARES CORPORATE BOND INDEX CLASS H - ACCUMULATION (GBP)	0.11%	GB00BJL5BV43
iShares Corporate Bond Index (UK) D Acc	0.11%	GB00B84DSW83
Fidelity Index Sterling Corporate Bond Fund P GBP Acc	0.12%	GB00BKX8GD57
UK Invm Grd Bd Idx £ Acc	0.12%	IE00B1S74Q32
"Legal & General Sterling Corporate Bond Index Fund "	0.14%	GB00B4M01C47
Sterling Corporate Bond Index fund	0.15%	GB00BYV9WC94
UBS STERLING CORPORATE BOND INDEXED CLASS C - ACCUMULATION (GROSS GBP)	0.17%	GB00B95J1785
SPDR® Bloomberg Sterling Corporate Bond UCITS ETF (UKCO)	0.20%	IE00B4694Z11

Global corporate bonds funds

Fund	OCF	ISIN
L&G ESG GBP Corporate Bond UCITS ETF	0.09%	IE00BLRPQM83
ISHARES OVERSEAS CORPORATE BOND INDEX CLASS H - ACCUMULATION (GBP)	0.11%	GB00BPFJD529
iShares Overseas Government Bond Index Fund (UK) Class D Acc GBP	0.11%	GB00B849C803
iShares ESG Overseas Corporate Bond Index Fund (UK) Class D Acc GBP	0.10%	GB00B58YKH53
Invesco USD Corporate Bond ESG UCITS ETF GBP Hedged (PUIP)	0.12%	IE00BJ06C481
Sterling Corporate Bond Index Fund	0.15%	GB00BYV9WC94
Global Bond Index Fund	0.15%	IE00B50W2R13
Global Corporate Bond Index Fund	0.18%	IE00BDFB5M56
abrdn Global Corporate Bond Tracker Fund B Acc	0.18%	GB00BF473024
iShares Global Corp Bond UCITS ETF	0.20%	IE00BFM6TB42
iShares Global Corp Bond UCITS ETF USD (Dist) (CRPS)	0.20%	IE00B7J7TB45

UK all shares funds

Fund	OCF	ISIN
ISHARES UK EQUITY INDEX CLASS D - ACCUMULATION (GBP)	0.05%	GB00B7C44X99
iShares UK Equity Index Fund (UK) H Acc	0.05%	GB00BPFJDB84
FIDELITY INDEX UK CLASS P - ACCUMULATION (GBP)	0.06%	GB00BJS8SF95
HSBC FTSE ALL SHARE INDEX CLASS C - ACCUMULATION (GBP)	0.06%	GB00B80QFX11
FTSE U.K. All Share Index Unit Trust	0.06%	GB00B3X7QG63
LEGAL & GENERAL UK INDEX CLASS C - ACCUMULATION (GBP)	0.11%	GB00BG0QPJ30
Invesco Markets II plc - Invesco FTSE All Share ESG Climate UCITS ETF (FASE)	0.12%	IE00BN7J5Z03
L&G (N) Tracker Trust	0.15%	GB00B8386G47
ABRDN UK ALL SHARE TRACKER CLASS B - ACCUMULATION (GBP)	0.17%	GB00B76B9Y24

"Aviva Investors UK Index Tracking Fund 2 GBP Inc"	0.20%	GB00B8XCGM21
SPDR® FTSE UK All Share UCITS ETF Acc (FTAL)	0.20%	IE00B7452L46

Global shares funds

Fund	OCF	ISIN
Amundi Index Solutions - Amundi Prime Global UCITS ETF DR (PRIW)	0.05%	LU1931974692
L&G Global Equity UCITS EFT	0.10%	IE00BFXR5S54
FIDELITY INDEX WORLD CLASS P - ACCUMULATION (GBP)	0.12%	GB00BJS8SJ34
SPDR® MSCI World UCITS ETF	0.12%	IE00BFY0GT14
FTSE Developed World UCITS ETF (VHVG)	0.12%	IE00BK5BQV03
L&G International Index I Acc	0.13%	GB00B2Q6HW61
L&G Global Equity Index I Acc	0.13%	GB00B83LW328
HSBC FTSE ALL WORLD INDEX CLASS C - ACCUMULATION (GBP)	0.13%	GB00BMJJJF91
FTSE Developed World ex-U.K. Equity Index Fund	0.14%	GB00B59G4Q73
HSBC MSCI World UCITS ETF (HMWO)	0.15%	IE00B4X9L533
iShares MSCI ACWI UCITS ETF	0.20%	IE00B6R52259
iShares Core MSCI World UCITS ETF USD (Acc) (SWDA)	0.20%	IE00B4L5Y983

Alternatives

Fund	OCF	ISIN
LEGAL & GENERAL GLOBAL REAL ESTATE DIVIDEND INDEX	0.16%	GB00BYW7CL14
"iShares Developed Real Estate Index Fund (IE) Class D GBP"	0.17%	GB00B5BFJG71
LEGAL & GENERAL GLOBAL INFRASTRUCTURE INDEX	0.20%	GB00BF0TZL74
"iShares Developed Real Estate Index Fund (IE) Class D GBP"	0.24%	IE00BKPWSS48
HSBC FTSE EPRA NAREIT Developed UCITS ETF (HPRO)	0.24%	IE00B5L01S80
"Legal & General Global Infrastructure Index Fund "	0.30%	GB00BF0TZG22
SPDR® Dow Jones Global Real Estate UCITS ETF (GBRE)	0.40%	IE00B8GF1M35
SPDR® Morningstar Multi-Asset Global Infrastructure UCITS ETF (GIN)	0.40%	IE00BQWJFQ70
iShares UK Property UCITS ETF	0.40%	IE00B1TXLS18
iShares US Property Yield UCITS ETF	0.40%	IE00B1FZSF77

Gold

Fund	OCF	ISIN
iShares Physical Gold ETC (SGLN)	0.12%	IE00B4ND3602
Amundi Physical Gold ETC C (GLDA)	0.12%	FR0013416716
Invesco Physical Gold ETC (SGLP)	0.12%	IE00B579F325

A3

Useful resources

Books

The Naked Trader by Robbie Burns

This is an excellent introduction to stock-picking (choosing specific companies to invest in). If that's your bag, this is your book.

The Little Book of Common Sense Investing by John C. Bogle

John Bogle was the chap who started the first passive fund in the 1970s. While everyone around him derided him and sought to continue making hundreds of millions for themselves, he persisted and led a revolution that has benefited ordinary investors like you and me. Hats off and thank you to the late, great Mr. Bogle.

Anything by Len Deighton, Martin Cruz-Smith, Robert Harris, Abir Mukherjee or Philip Kerr.

These authors have produced a load of really good thrillers, murder mysteries and spy novels. Nothing to do with investments but, because of the way I've set up my investments, I have time to indulge my reading habits. Ideal with a cup of freshly ground coffee and a hot croissant. Just saying.

Websites

Invest Without Being Ripped Off

My own website, created to accompany this book, which provides updates, insights and the returns and costs on the investments I set up in this book.

InvestWithoutBeingRippedOff.com

Age UK

This excellent charity has some really useful information on pensions and annuities including a video from the excellent host of BBC Radio 4's Moneybox, Paul Lewis.
https://www.ageuk.org.uk/information-advice/money-legal/pensions/annuities/

Bank of England's banking licence list

Up to £85,000 of your money might be covered by the government guarantee referred to as the Financial Services Compensation Scheme (FSCS).

This web document provides a list of banking licences in the UK. Each banking licence can mean a guarantee of up to £85,000 of your money under companies covered by that licence.

Each licence might include different companies (for example Clydesdale, Virgin and Yorkshire Bank) but an aggregate total of £85,000 of your money across all three of those companies would be covered. If you have, say, £50,000 in Clydesdale and £50,000 in Virgin, you'd only be covered for £85,000 of that £100,000 total.

https://www.bankofengland.co.uk/-/media/boe/files/prudential-regulation/authorisations/which-firms-does-the-pra-regulate/2022/list-of-banking-brands-july-2022.pdf

Debt advice websites

Money Helper (formerly Money Advice Service) - www.moneyhelper.org.uk/
National Debt Line - www.nationaldebtline.org/
Citizens Advice Bureau – www.citizensadvice.org.uk/debt-and-money/
Step Change - www.stepchange.org/

Financial Conduct Authority's (FCA) assessment of fund managers

The FCA's damning report on how fund managers treat their customers.
www.fca.org.uk/publications/multi-firm-reviews/authorised-fund-managers-assessments-their-funds-value

Financial Conduct Authority's (FCA) investment data report

The report I refer to in which active fund fees are reported as averaging 0.89% a year as opposed to an average of just 0.15% a year for passive funds (the ones I like are cheaper).
www.fca.org.uk/data/investment-management-data-annual-report-2020-21

Financial Services Compensation Scheme (FSCS)

This is the government guarantee of your money if the company you hold it with goes bust.
www.fscs.org.uk

Investopedia

An explanation of loads of financial terms and bits of jargon.
www.investopedia.com

MoneyMagpie

Advice and information on making money, saving money and dealing with debt.
www.MoneyMapgie.com

The Naked Trader

A fully clothed Robbie Burns shares his excellent insights on stock-picking and spread betting for those of you who want to dive into that sort of type of investing.
www.NakedTrader.co.uk

Risk assessment questionnaire (Academic original)

The questionnaire created by John Grable and Ruth Lytton as visiting professors at the University of Missouri on which I've based the risk questionnaire in this book.
https://pfp.missouri.edu/research/investment-risk-tolerance-assessment/

UK government ISA resource

Starting point for all sorts of government info on UK Individual Savings Accounts (ISAs)
www.gov.uk/individual-savings-accounts

UK government pension resource

Starting point for all sorts of government info on UK pensions
www.gov.uk/personal-pension-your-rights

UK government Check Your State Pension resource

www.gov.uk/check-state-pension

UK pension annual allowance checking tool

The HMRC resource that does what it says on the tin.
www.hmrc.gov.uk/tools/pension-allowance/

Unbiased (IFAs)

Independent Financial Advisor UK IFA database
www.ifa.org.uk

Underperforming their own benchmarks

The S&P Dow Jones Indices LLP report on how bad active fund managers are at hitting the very targets they set for themselves.
www.spglobal.com/spdji/en/documents/spiva/spiva-us-year-end-2020.pdf

Index